Presented To:

_____

From:

_____

Date:

_____

GLORY INVASION

BOOKS BY DAVID HERZOG

Living in the Glory Every Day

Desperate for New Wine

Mysteries of the Glory Unveiled

The Ancient Portals of Heaven

AVAILABLE FROM DESTINY IMAGE PUBLISHERS

GLORY INVASION

Walking Under an Open Heaven

DAVID HERZOG

Expanded Edition with Devotional

DESTINY IMAGE® PUBLISHERS, INC.

P.O. Box 310, Shippensburg, PA 17257-0310

"Promoting Inspired Lives."

This book and all other Destiny Image, Revival Press, MercyPlace, Fresh Bread, Destiny Image Fiction, and Treasure House books are available at Christian bookstores and distributors worldwide.

For a U.S. bookstore nearest you, call 1-800-722-6774.

For more information on foreign distributors, call 717-532-3040.

Reach us on the Internet: www.destinyimage.com.

ISBN 13 TP: 978-0-7684-4099-7

ISBN 13 Ebook: 978-0-7684-8867-8

For Worldwide Distribution, Printed in the U.S.A.

3 4 5 6 7 8 / 16 15 14 13 12

DEDICATION

The original *Glory Invasion* book was dedicated to the Creator of Heaven and earth from whom I received the revelations, the direction, and the strength to finish it in the midst of our travels to more than 30 countries in the past few years. I dedicate this expanded version to Him as well. Without God, I would not be where I am today. He is the source of everything good, and saying "yes" to follow Him has been my greatest decision and adventure.

The book and devotional is also dedicated to Stephanie, my wife, who has stood by my side, prayed for me, taken huge steps of faith along with me, and encouraged me to write. She is a beautiful woman inside and out—full of God's glory. She is my best friend and the love of my life who has traveled all around the world with me and has been my constant source of encouragement. She has ventured with me into the deep realms of the glory of God, the most exciting adventure a couple could ever experience together—increasing our love for each other and God.

I also dedicate this book to my three little angels: Tiffany Joy, Shannon Glory, and Destiny Shalom, our daughters. They are gifts from God beyond what we could have ever asked or imagined—so full of glory and multigifted. They have survived and even thrived while traveling worldwide and ministering along with us. They bring the greatest joy and love that a father could ever ask for. Our daughters motivate me to go past the limits, breaking into new spiritual territory for the next generation.

ACKNOWLEDGMENTS

Special thanks to all our intercessors, friends, and partners, who pray and fast over every e-mail we send out, and those who prayed for the completion and favor over the original book and this expanded version. Thank you, too, to those who have given support for this ministry so that the glory of God can be presented worldwide.

I gratefully acknowledge Mahesh and Bonnie Chavda, who have been mentors, friends, and faithful examples of living in the glory.

I would like to acknowledge the late Ruth Ward Heflin, who has been the greatest inspiration of living in the glory. The love she showed us by taking us under her wing in a sense by inviting us to be part of her life and to minister alongside her for the short time we knew her totally revolutionized our lives.

Special thanks to Sid Roth for his friendship and the impartation he released to us to reach God's chosen people in a much greater way.

ENDORSEMENT

David Herzog is a man who had a "Saul of Tarsus experience" to explain the dynamics of the invisible world. Miracles are normal when we live in God's Kingdom. As you read this book, the supernatural world becomes your normal.

SID ROTH
Host, *It's Supernatural!* television program

CONTENTS

FOREWORD

I first met David about ten years ago at the funeral of Ruth Heflin, a mutual friend of ours, where we were seated together. Little did I know that soon after we would be ministering together both in the United States and overseas. David has also ministered at our conferences in Charlotte and has been an enormous blessing. I ministered at David's conference in Paris, France, on two occasions and was blessed to see the impact of his work in Europe while he and his wife, Stephanie, were based there. Besides his campaigns and conferences, his ministry has been very valuable to many local churches as revival has erupted, thus equipping many congregations across the country and around the world.

The glory of God manifests in David's meetings with creative miracles that flow freely. David is constantly pressing in to new realms of God's anointing. This is one of the reasons for the unusual miracles, fresh revelation, prophetic accuracy, and salvations that regularly occur in his meetings.

David, along with his family, has become a family friend. More than anything else, it's our mutual love for the presence and glory of God that has bonded our families together. He has been a modern-day pioneer in taking the presence and power of God past the limits most have set, and seeing God manifest in new ways.

If you are hungry to take the glory of God to the next level in your life, then get ready to have your life transformed and blessed as you take a quantum leap into *Glory Invasion*.

Dr. Mahesh Chavda
Senior Pastor, All Nations Church
Charlotte, North Carolina

INTRODUCTION

The spirit of Elijah is appearing in our generation as it was prophesied it would in the last days: *"Behold, I will send you Elijah the prophet before the coming of the great and dreadful day of the Lord"* (Mal. 4:5). We are beginning to see the signs, wonders, and miracle ministry restored to the way it was in the days of Elijah and Jesus.

During His time on earth, Jesus restored this glory to Israel with miracles and signs that had not been seen for centuries. Many even asked, "Are You Elijah?" Why would they think He was Elijah resurrected? Basically because He did the same things Elijah did—He raised the dead, performed signs and wonders over nature and people, and commanded the wind and waves to stop.

Similarly, Elijah commanded the rain to stop for three and a half years. Jesus multiplied the bread just as Elijah, who also multiplied the widow's food. Jesus confronted the government authorities of Rome and the religious establishment—as did Elijah, who confronted King Ahab and the priests of Baal.

After Jesus ascended, He sent the Holy Spirit to His followers, and a glory invasion began. But not until they prayed, *"And now Lord…grant to Your bond servants [full freedom] to declare Your message fearlessly, while You stretch out Your hand to cure and to perform signs and wonders…"* (Acts 4:29-30 AMP). This is the beginning of the fullness of His glory released upon the early church. When they prayed in this way, they saw the dawn of a greater glory operate—as in the signs and wonders of Jesus and Elijah.

Immediately after praying, the building shakes and the first signs begin. Even financial miracles eliminate poverty from the church, *"nor was there anyone among them who lacked...*" (Acts 4:34). We also see them testifying to the resurrection of the Lord, and raising the dead takes place again. As Peter walks by, even his shadow heals the sick.

Unfortunately, most of the church today is missing this fullness of the glory. Most of us are stuck living in Acts 2—when the Holy Spirit fell. Many of us speak in tongues, lay hands on the sick, and often see people added to the church. But what we need to bring about a *Glory Invasion* is an Acts 4 outpouring to reap Acts 4 results. The Pentecost outpouring is fine, but a new level of glory and power came after the Acts 2 outpouring. Many want the results of Acts 4 power and glory without moving beyond Acts 2. You need an Acts 4 visitation to have an Acts 4 manifestation of revival and glory.

We need to get on our faces and cry out for a whole new visitation of glory as the apostles did and pray for the new glory to be accompanied with signs, wonders, and miracles, as Jesus promised it would be. This is the beginning of the apostolic anointing that many talk about yet lack the power to walk in. In my book, *Mysteries of the Glory Unveiled,* how the glory operates and manifests is explained. I also describe the next level and how to take glory to the extreme.

I believe we are about to enter a new season in church history—a phase that goes beyond the initial Pentecost experience of being filled with the Spirit. We are entering a phase that will cause us to challenge the very powers holding back the advance of the church. When this glory invasion is fully realized, it will usher in a supernatural acceleration of the things of God. Elijah prophesied during a time of famine that the rains would come. (See First Kings 18:1-2,41.) Once God had spoken, the prophecy and declaration alone caused it to come forth. *Prophetically declaring the new thing God has shown us is the first step.* Without taking this initial step of obedience, the other steps are in vain.

When we declare something under the direction of God, that thing is being created as we declare it. Just as when God declared in Genesis 1:3, *"Let there be light,"* instantly there was light. The lack of prophetic declaration hinders the creation and birthing of those things into existence. This is why we cannot do without the prophetic.

The Church is built upon the prophetic and apostolic nature of God. In essence, God allows us to create life and bring things into existence by the prophetic word.

After declaring the word, sometimes we must also enter into prayer or intercession as Elijah did. He got down and put himself into a birthing position and prayed until it came (see 1 Kings 18:42). The prophecy was what gave life to it and the intercession caused it to grow until birth. The final step was when he started to look for the prophecy. He told his servant to look until he saw something. Once you declare and pray through, you must simply enter into it. He looked seven times until he saw the "sign"—a cloud the size of a man's hand, and then Elijah ran. He girded up his loins, the Bible says, and outran the chariot. (See First Kings 18:43-46.) When the Church lays hold of these truths, even governments will open their ears once again to "hear the Word of the Lord."

As you read this book, God will supernaturally reveal the new glory to you and allow you to catch up, even if you feel you are behind in knowing these things. Ask God now to help you understand what He is doing on the earth today. Now is the time to run, as the first signs have already appeared heralding the new outpouring. As Elijah did, gird up your loins and run so as not to miss the next move of God. Don't casually walk toward it, but run so you don't miss it.

Some of us may feel like our ministry focuses on repentance, intercession, praise, giving, preaching, the prophetic, or evangelism, etc. We tend to specialize in one area, master it, and stay in that anointing indefinitely. God wants a convergence of these anointings that will cause one big explosion of His glory. When you mix a certain combination of gases together, you can create a bomb. God is combining a mixture that will cause the church to become a dangerous weapon against the enemy in these last days. Prepare for a *Glory Invasion!*

SECTION I

SOUND
AND
GLORY

CHAPTER ONE

THE GLORY ZONE

*By faith we understand that the worlds were framed by
the word of God, so that the things which are seen were
not made of things which are visible* (Hebrews 11:3).

I have always wondered how God could have created everything out
of nothing. Although I have totally believed the Creation account
from my earliest youth, I never quite understood how this could be. I
knew that if one day I could understand how God created something
out of seemingly nothing, then we could also use the same principles
to see the creative handiwork of God again in our day.

It says in the Scriptures that everything that was made was made
of things that are not visible. It does not say that God created everything out of nothing. It simply states what *kind* of things He used—
invisible things. The more I meditated on this Scripture, the more the
entire Creation account made perfect sense.

The writer of Hebrews clearly says, *"Things which are seen were not
made of things which are visible."* So what are these invisible things that
He used to create everything?

Genesis 1 gives clues:

*In the beginning God created the heavens and the earth. The
earth was without form, and void; and darkness was on the
face of the deep. And the Spirit of God was hovering over the
face of the waters* (Genesis 1:1-2).

The first invisible thing God sent was His own Spirit or Glory upon the earth. The first ingredient is the Glory. Once you are in a *glory zone* anything is possible. God used His own Spirit as the first major ingredient that is not visible. The next ingredient is sound: *"Then God said, 'Let there be light'; and there was light"* (Gen. 1:3).

Suddenly, God Almighty the Creator spoke—BANG!—greater than a sonic boom ripping across time and space. This is the *real* "Big Bang" theory—God spoke and *bang!*

Only God's voice could have created everything, since nothing was created before this. So the second invisible ingredient is sound or "sound waves," as scientists call them. God spoke and everything was created. How did sound create the earth and stars and then everything else in the same manner by God simply declaring them to be created? After the atmosphere of the glory and presence of God was on the earth, all God had to do was speak into His own cloud of His glory.

When you are in the *glory zone* and speak out what God is telling or showing you, things will start to be created at that moment. I will explain how this occurs behind the scenes. There is a difference between saying words flippantly as opposed to prophetically declaring with conviction those same words when you are in a zone or atmosphere of His glory. He is the Creator, so if you follow the same pattern of waiting for His glory to come and then speak out what He is saying, the same things will follow.

The unseen or invisible *things* that God used to create are His presence and sound waves. Even God was never recorded as opening His mouth to speak anything until first He sent His own Spirit or Glory to first hover, creating an atmosphere conducive to creative miracles. Everything created was created using that part of God Himself, His Spirit, to create it. Without the element of God's Spirit hovering, nothing else can be created; He is the only Creator.

This is how Elijah could command rain to fall or not, and how Ezekiel could command dead, dry human bones to come back together (see Ezek. 37:1-8). First these men of God immersed themselves in the Spirit or Glory of God and then they spoke, prophesied, or declared what God told them to speak. But what actually happens behind the scenes to cause these things to occur?

E=MC²

Even Einstein's theory of relativity connects to the Creation story. Albert Einstein (1879–1955) was a Jewish scientist who thoroughly studied the first five books of the Bible, which most Jews of his day knew well. As a scientist, he was especially fascinated by the Creation account. His theory in simplified terms: E is energy and M is mass or substance. Basically, Einstein concluded that energy is real, even though it is invisible to the naked eye. One example of energy is electricity. Though you cannot see it, you know it is real when you turn on a light or turn off the television.

Energy can also be experienced through the presence, glory, and Spirit of God. When the presence of God is felt during a time of worship, often you become energized not just spiritually but physically as well—even though you may have been exhausted only moments earlier. Suddenly, because of His presence, you are filled with physical and spiritual energy.

The presence of God's glory releases a supernatural energy and provides the potential for miracles. Energy is substance, even if your eye cannot yet see it. The presence, power, Spirit and Glory of God is not an emotion that only those who are sensitive can feel. Energy is a power, a capacity for work—just like electricity and sound waves that you can't see, but still exist.

An example is John G. Lake, a great missionary to South Africa in the early 1900s. In his account, many people in South Africa were dying of disease. While assisting doctors during a bubonic plague outbreak, Lake was asked why he had not contracted the disease, since he used no protection. He said, "It is the Spirit of life in Christ Jesus." To demonstrate, he had them take live bubonic plague germs still foaming from the lungs of a newly dead person and put them in his hands, and then examine the germs under a microscope. The germs were dead![1]

The energy and presence of God was invisible to the naked eye but magnified under the microscope's lens—there proved to be a real, formidable, existing power that killed the virus. This is how John G. Lake explained why he did not get sick—he carried the cure in his body and spirit to heal disease through the power of the Spirit through Jesus.

In another amazing testimony, John G. Lake asked doctors to bring him a man with inflammation in the bone. He asked them to take their instruments and attach it to his leg while he prayed for healing. Then he asked them what they saw taking place on their instruments. They replied that every cell was responding positively! John G. Lake replied, "That is God's divine science!"[2]

SOUND WAVES

Some scientists (especially those who work in string theory) believe that the smallest particle is not the electron, the neutron, or the proton—it is sound, "sound waves" or vibrating strings that have "notes."[3] When you take a tiny subatomic particle (a neutron or a proton) and split it to its smallest form, there is one more particle inside the subatomic particle—a vibrating sound wave. If this is true, and if the Genesis account in which God used His words, or sound, to create is true, then I believe that sound waves are the smallest living substance unseen by the human eye that is at the core of every created thing.

The Scriptures confirm this, stating that *"the very stones will cry out"* (Luke 19:40 AMP). If sound waves are imbedded in every created thing, this would confirm the Genesis account: every living thing was created when God spoke it all into existence. So there are sound waves imbedded in every created thing.

Man was created from the dust. The Hebrew word for "dust" is *aphar*, and it does not mean dirt. It actually means, "smallest created particle." I believe that the smallest particle is a sound wave, the building block and first ingredient of all things created—including man. It is now being studied through experiments by Japanese researcher Masaru Emoto that water particles and other subatomic particles actually respond to sound and even voice recognition.[4] If this is true, then every created thing can hear in a sense and respond in some way, as all things created were first created with the same core ingredients—sound and the glory or the presence of God.

In Psalm 148 God commands the sun, moon, and stars to praise Him. He even commands mountains and hills to praise Him. Only an intelligent God who knows His creation intimately can command seemingly inanimate objects to respond in worship to Him. In fact, all creation has the ability to hear, listen, obey, respond, and worship its Creator. Jesus commanded the fig tree to die after not producing fruit, and the tree obeyed Him. Every living thing can and does respond. Quantum physics confirms that if you study an object long enough, it will respond in a certain way because you were observing it; thus it realizes it is being observed.

NASA scientists recently discovered that sound waves of musical harmonious notes were coming from black holes[5] (collapsed stars) and other experiments revealed similar results from rock samples taken from outer space.[6] In fact, they found that all created things have musical sound waves imbedded in them.

Why would musical sounds be produced from His creation? The Lord commands everything to worship Him. Hence, rock samples from distant planets emit sounds of worship that we can hear when put under special machines that track sound waves and energy.

Have you ever noticed that when you are traveling alone in the countryside, walking in the woods, or enjoying a beautiful natural setting you often sense the presence of God? Have you noticed that at times when you are attending a church retreat camp or something similar in natural surroundings you seem to receive a greater touch from God? Creation emits "sound waves of worship" that are invisible to your natural ear, but your spirit receives them.

Jesus and Elijah often went out to the mountain, John went to the desert, and Moses climbed up the mountain to get alone with God. Have you noticed that you often can connect with God more easily in beautiful natural surroundings? I believe that all creation in its natural state is worshiping the Creator. Praise and worship brings the presence of God. There is an ongoing symphony praising Him 24/7 in nature, in His uncorrupted creation. Your spirit feels refreshed, and you often feel closer to God in nature than you do in the city, where the creation is no longer in its raw, natural state.

Often we listen to music and worship tapes to help us get into the presence of God. But when you are outdoors, you sense His presence without manmade music because there is a natural ongoing orchestra of worship via the creation. Even though your natural ear cannot hear it, this invisible worship welcomes the presence of God.

When people pray against cancer, they often command the disease to go as if it is a person. Also, people pray and command their broken bones to be healed. I used to think it was strange to talk to sickness in this way; but this is possible because every created thing has sound waves and responds to sound waves spoken with the Glory and Spirit of God. Just saying words or reciting Scriptures is not the key. The letter of the law kills, but the Spirit gives life. Get into the *glory zone* of His presence first, then speak forth and the creation will respond to your word—if it is attached to the Spirit.

Even cancer responds to the sound and command of your spoken words! I believe that if you speak to the cancer while in the presence of God, and in faith, believing and understanding that the cancer can hear you and respond, it will die. I have seen this occur countless times. Now even doctors use sound waves to treat cancer. Doctors use a procedure called high-intensity focused ultrasound, which is high-energy sound waves, to destroy cancer cells.[7] The high-intensity words you speak to the cancer cells that can hear and respond are much more powerful with the Holy Spirit and Glory.

So if created objects can respond because they themselves have sound emanating from them, then God is showing us more of how He operated through Jesus and the prophets. When Jesus commanded the fig tree to whither, it obeyed because it was created with the capacity to hear and obey. Objects such as rocks, mountains, and trees communicate with and worship God—all of His creation not only hears and understands but also replies and worships Him. This being true, the creation also can respond to you when you speak words of faith directed by God in the glory realm.

Now you know why Jesus said we could speak to a mountain and it is possible for it to be removed (see Matt. 17:20). The disciples also marveled that even *"winds and water...obey Him"* (Luke 8:25). It is not just diseases but also creation itself that obeys. This realization opens a whole new world of authority over creation. God told Moses to speak to the rock and it would produce water. Satan tempted Jesus in the desert to command the stones to turn to bread. Satan knew it was entirely possible for Jesus to perform the miracle. But Jesus did not succumb because He was fasting and would not take orders from or be tempted by satan. Empowering Moses to turn a rock into water is not much different from Jesus' ability to turn stones into bread. Often when praying for miracles, we command broken bones to reconnect. The bones can hear and respond just as all created things can. Body parts and creation can hear and respond.

GLORY INVASION MIRACLES

Why and how is this possible? In the biblical account of Creation, God spoke for the first time in recorded history in Genesis 1:3, *"'Let there be light'; and there was light."* Accordingly, everything was created with sound directing it to be a certain thing. First the Spirit began to hover over the waters, then sound was released. So if you are in the presence of God, it is also possible to redirect an object to be another created thing. If the original raw materials that created a certain object are present (the Spirit of God, as revealed in Genesis), then sound can redirect the same created object into another form—especially if you are in the glory realm of God where the Spirit is hovering.

I believe that nothing created can be uncreated—things created only change form; even according to the first law of thermodynamics this is known to be true. For example, burned wood turns to ash but does not disappear. Although the ash seems to dissolve, it is reduced to smaller molecules that still contain imbedded sound particles. Consequently, one created object can turn into another created thing if directed by sound waves or a command under the direction of the Holy Spirit.

When Moses threw his rod down and it turned into a serpent, the Pharaoh's magicians were able to do the same thing. This proves that the miracle or act of turning something into something else is not wrong or evil in and of itself. The important questions are: Who is the source of the miracle? Whose power is in operation? Jesus could have easily turned the stones into bread but Jesus would not have turned the stones to bread by satan's command because the source would have changed. Jesus' only source is His Father in Heaven. His first miracle turned water into wine. Again we see one created form turning into another. I believe we will start to see the renewal of these types of miracles take place again in the days ahead when we will have authority over creation, have the faith and revelation to see things created change forms, and show the magicians and sorcerers of our day who God really is.

So if we have faith to see an object turn into another object, how much easier is it to see things created multiply themselves? Everything generally produces after its own kind. The fish and the loaves easily multiplied at Jesus' command (see Matt. 14:17-21). I have experienced special miracles like this. Someone planned a party for me after church one Sunday. The hostess had made exactly 23 sandwiches and two pitchers of water because she only invited a handful of people. For some reason though, half the church showed up. The lady who prepared the food was shocked. God told her to quiet down and believe for a miracle. She did, and during the event she watched at least 30 to 40 people eat at least two or three sandwiches each. At the end of the party, there were sandwiches left over. The two pitchers of drink should have provided enough for one serving for each person, but she had enough to refill each glass—God had multiplied the drinks too!

Another time, we were holding a large evangelistic miracle crusade in a big auditorium in Paris, France. It was very expensive to rent such a place. When we counted all the offerings given by believers during the outreach, we ran short of what we needed to pay for the crusade expenses. The Lord told me to tell the counters to keep counting. As they did, the bills suddenly multiplied. I told them to keep counting until they came to a certain amount that was enough to cover all the expenses. We ended up with above and beyond what we needed, as God had supernaturally multiplied the finances. We have seen this miracle many times over.

We also are witnessing many people receive instant weight loss during our meetings. One man in Tennessee lost 70 pounds in one service after receiving a word of knowledge. In Las Vegas during the first night of meetings, about 20 women lost weight equal to five dress sizes. God can just as easily remove fat cells as we can put them on. As you start to meditate on this revelation and on how big God really is, you will begin to believe and then you will see these same miracles happen in your own life.

We have witnessed many financial miracles and debt cancellations in our meetings as well. After people have given to the work of God, because of the creative miracle realm they notice money miracles happen very quickly. Some even find money in their pockets and purses immediately after placing an offering in the basket. Others have discovered thousands of dollars in their bank accounts that were not there before. God performed the same miracles: multiplying resources for the widow, feeding the crowd with loaves and fish, prospering Peter with many fish, placing the gold coin in a fish's mouth to pay the taxes—and there are many more examples of God's glorious provision miracles.

In our meetings we are seeing more and more bald people receive instant hair growth. A lady in Prescott, Arizona, received hair growth while we were all watching! We actually saw her bald spots filling in with hair. In Augusta, Georgia, hair appeared instantly on top of a man's head where he was totally bald, and the color of his new hair was its original dark color. We have also seen people with white hair have their hair returned to its original color. It is amazing to watch these transformations.

So if everything created cannot be destroyed but can only be converted into another form, then the hair still exists somewhere—it has just been converted to another form, but it still exists. There is no distance in the glory, so wherever your hair is, it can still respond. And because your hair has sound waves and can hear and respond, when I am in the glory zone in a meeting I can call out, "Hair, come back." It can return to its original state and respond to my words spoken under the direction of the Holy Spirit. God cares about every hair on your head (see Luke 12:7); how much more He cares for the pressing needs and problems in your life.

How do you think Ezekiel was able to prophesy and speak to bones and say, *"O dry bones, hear the word of the Lord!"* (Ezek. 37:4-6)? God was telling him to speak to bones—not demons, people, God, or angels, but bones! And when he did, they responded as proof that they could hear and obey. Then even the sinews and flesh joined in and reformed. How could the flesh that was dissolved return? Again, nothing created is really gone, it only changes form into smaller molecules and atoms we cannot see. At the sound of God's command, they are reformed. Ezekiel even prophesied over the dry bone's breath, which is their spirit when translated from the original, and it also obeyed and returned. How would the bones know which bones to reconnect to after so many years? Apparently created things have a memory just as we have a memory.

At a health clinic in Mexico, an organic garden field was cultivated and maintained normally, except that the owner told the gardeners to show lots of love, care, and attention to the plants growing in only in half of the garden. At the end of the growing season, the half of the garden that was treated kindly produced twice as many crops as the other half.

In another experiment at the same clinic, a man had two trees growing in front of his window. He projected hate and anger toward one tree and to the other he expressed love. In six weeks the tree that received hate and anger withered and almost died; the other tree flourished. Creation responds to what humans say and do.[8]

The Bible says the earth swallowed up Korah and those who joined in his rebellion. It is possible that the earth where he was standing got tired of his sin and rebellion. (See Numbers 16:32.) I believe that there are geographical locations on the earth where sin has reached such a high level that the earth, waves, and the elements have turned against man, as they can no longer tolerate the enormity of filth. This will become more and more evident in the last days, as sin abounds in certain cities more than others, and where there is not enough light to counteract the darkness. The Bible even says that the creation itself groans with birth pangs for the manifestation of the sons and daughters of God. (See Romans 8:19,22.)

IF WALLS COULD TALK

I led a tour to Israel recently, and our friend, a missionary pastor, was with us. He had been struggling for eight years with the idea that Israel has a special place in God's heart. He grew up on replacement theology, and no matter what Scriptures he read that showed him how God was still dealing with the Jewish people, he could not get the revelation. But he did see the effects and blessings of those who pray for and love Israel and the Jewish people. He decided to go to Israel for understanding and insight.

The first day we visited the Western Wall in Jerusalem. At the wall, the pastor leaned his head against it and prayed. Within minutes he broke out in great tears and weeping. This was very unusual for him, as his personality was more reserved and analytical, especially concerning Israel. After the incident he told me that somehow at the wall he suddenly understood the last 3,000 years of Jewish history and began to accept Israel's place in the end times. I was surprised that he so quickly changed his mind after leaning against the wall for only a few minutes—after all, I had been explaining the subject to him for eight years.

But the wall offered thousands of years of witness to things that had occurred, including Jesus' teachings and healings, the temple cleansing, the last supper with the disciples, the persecution, the empty tomb. They had been there all along, and the sound waves were still emanating from the rock wall—not only worshiping, but explaining the true story of God's covenant people and why they are here today. The walls spoke to his spirit and downloaded 3,000 years of history and revelation to him. Again, if created objects can emit sound waves of worship to God, who is a Spirit, then it is also possible for our spirit to pick up those same sound waves that are still resonating off of created objects and also bringing revelation about things from the past!

Recently, after sharing this revelation, the following story was told to me. A little girl was having nightmares while sleeping in her bedroom. The family had just moved into the house, and the girl never had nightmares before. She was able to sleep peacefully in other rooms but not in her room, even after the family had prayed several times about it. In her bedroom, she kept having the same dream about a murder and how it happened. Finally, after praying, the parents decided to call the former homeowners and find out if there was anything unusual that occurred in that room. They were told that a murder actually had taken place in that room and it had happened exactly as the girl had seen it in her dream. The walls witnessed the murder and retold the story to the little girl in her dreams. The family prayed over the walls, commanding not only the spirit of murder to leave, but also the memory of what happened there to be washed away by the blood of Jesus.

The blood of the sin of murder was crying out in that situation. The Bible mentions that the blood of the martyrs is crying out. (See Genesis 4:10.) The actual blood of the martyrs speaks—not just the martyrs, but also their blood. Again we realize that all things have a voice, and their sound can be carried over time to be experienced again.

Just as an object can carry on it the weight and presence of God—as Paul's handkerchief, Samson's jawbone of a donkey, and Moses' rod—it can also carry memories of the past and both good and evil things that are part of it. After Elisha died, his bones still had the power, glory, and sound of God emanating from them. A dead man was thrown over Elisha's bones in a grave and the dead man was resurrected, as the glory still resided in those bones, possibly many years after his death. (See Second Kings 13:21.)

We have prayed over objects and saturated them with the power of God. During a crusade I was conducting, two crippled people got up and walked after a simple word from God. Another crippled man left the meeting early. His wife drove him to the hotel, and as she was picking up the keys inside the hotel, a man stole the car with the crippled man in it. The thief pushed the man out of the moving car and the seat belt caught around his leg—tearing it from his body. He was found bleeding by the side of the road. The ambulance took him to the hospital emergency room and the doctors grafted the torn and already paralyzed leg back onto his body.

During the meeting that night after we saw the two crippled people walk, we prayed over the tissue boxes and saturated them with the same glory that was in the room and was causing the other miracles. People sent tissues to friends, who were healed after receiving them. One woman took a tissue to the man in the hospital and placed it on his mangled leg that the doctors had tried to regraft to his body. Suddenly he began to feel electricity run down his leg—totally amazing since he was paralyzed and his leg had just been reattached after being traumatically torn off. Soon he was wiggling his toes—another miracle. By the fifth day he was released from the hospital and able to walk! Although his leg had been dead weight from being crippled and the subsequent torn trauma, he could walk. God is amazing!

That is an awesome true story, but how did it happen? Well, if energy is equal to matter or mass, then that means the glory of God, which is supernatural power and energy, is also matter and has weight, even though you can't see it. When you saturate a tissue with the glory, substance, and weight of God, it will be heavier than before it was saturated—it will have weight that it did not have before. The object simply holds that same glory and then releases and transfers it when it is placed on someone by faith.

The glory can also be carried by invisible sound waves traveling through time and space. For example, when you watch a miracle crusade on television that was filmed three months previously and you get healed while watching it and feel the awesome presence of God, the glory has traveled through time and space to you. Even though you were not there when the actual crusade took place, whenever you watch it, the same glory is reactivated and you receive the same impartation, healing, or blessing as if you had been there three months ago. The glory of the meeting that took place at a particular time is frozen when taped and then unfrozen and reactivated the moment you watch it. So the voice waves of the one speaking, the worship, and the very atmosphere in that meeting can be contained in sound and light in the form of images and can be reactivated.

I once experimented with this belief. I was watching some never-before-seen footage of one of A.A. Allen's ministry meetings. Although the meeting had been taped 50 years previously, I could sense the same glory, power, and excitement in his voice—it seemed as if I was there. It was not just an emotional feeling, because I also felt the same glory. I watched as he pulled paralyzed people up out of wheelchairs. That night I was to preach in a revival meeting. A crippled woman came up to me, and almost without thinking and full of faith, I told her to stand up and walk. I took her hand and helped her up, and she walked for the first time! There was an impartation from a revival from the 1950s frozen in time, and waiting for me to receive it and release it by pushing the play button on the VCR.

ENDNOTES

1. Harold J. Chadwick, *How to Be Filled with Spiritual Power, Based on the Miracle Ministry of John G. Lake* (Orlando, FL: Bridge-Logos, 2006).

2. John G. Lake, *Adventures in God* (Tulsa, OK: Harrison House, 1991), 30.

3. Brian Greene, *The Elegant Universe* (New York: W.W. Norton & Company, 1999), 146.

4. Masaru Emoto, *The Hidden Messages in Water* (Hillsboro, OR: Beyond Words Publishing, 2004).

5. www.gsfc.nasa/scienceques2003/20031003.htmheadlinesy2003/09sep_blackholesounds.htm.

6. NASA Marshall Space Flight Center, "Chandra 'hears a black hole,'" news release (2003). http://www.nasa.gov/centers/marshall/news/news/releases/2003/03-152.html.

7. National Cancer Institute, www.cancer.gov/cancertopics/pdq/treatment/prostate/Patient/page4.

8. Kevin Trudeau, *Natural Cures* (Alliance Publishing), 267.

CHAPTER TWO

CREATIVE MIRACLES

For everyone who asks receives, and he who seeks finds,
and to him who knocks it will be opened (Luke 11:10).

In this next move of God we will begin to see extreme demonstrations of God's power and glory that will suspend the very laws of gravity. There have been many miracles that seem to defy the laws of nature and gravity. As the church delves into this area of God's glory invasion, I believe we will see more of these miracles in our day.

We know that everything was created by the glory of God and the sound or the spoken word. So when the heaviness of God's glory is present in a meeting, for example, we know that every body part and creative miracle needed is available. But how do you extract those creative miracles from the glory in the meeting? By realizing that all the miracles and body parts are in the glory—but in an expanded form. To illustrate, look at these four dots:

. .

. .

You can easily see these dots that are placed relatively closely to each other on the page. But imagine if I placed these same four dots in the four corners of a football stadium. You would know they are there but you would not be able to see them all at the same time, as the space between them would have been expanded over a larger area. Similarly, your body parts are in the meeting and the glory of God is present. You were created from His glory, so body parts are present but are suspended in the glory in an expanded form. The power is there for a miracle and the body parts are there; now we need to extract a particular body part from the glory realm that is in the room. You do so by declaring the body part to be made manifest and the parts to come together so you can see the miracle visibly, just as you can see the dots when they are in a compacted form.

The second ingredient for a creative miracle is sound or a spoken word commanding an object to form out of the raw material of the glory. We know from Chapter 1 that everything created can listen and obey, as it too is made of sound. We also know that nothing created can ever be destroyed but only changes form. Knowing this, you can command your hair or your cartilage to return and be reformed or recreated from the glory that is present. The body part has the capacity to obey. Accepting this revelation helps us pray with much greater faith and authority for creative miracles and body parts.

This realization is why we are witnessing instant weight loss in most of our meetings as we command fat cells to depart. Imagine if you commanded your fat cells to be stretched out as far as the east is from the west: you would no longer be able to see the fat. This is how a lot of creative miracles happen. We have also seen people's missing teeth, as well as hair, cartilage, and thyroids reappear, even after they have been surgically removed. We use the same Genesis 1:1-3 principle of how God created the earth and everything in it—including you and me.

If we only see God as the Healer and focus our preaching and receiving on healing, then we will only see healings, but not *creative miracles*. In order to see the creative we must see God as Creator as well. We must know God more as the Creator than as the Healer in order to abound in the creative miracles. The reason: God manifests the way you perceive Him. For example, some churches focus on the God of salvation and consequently they witness many salvations, but not healings. Other churches emphasize a God who delivers and He manifests as such. God will manifest in the way you perceive Him. Do not limit God—see Him in unlimited aspects and you will see unlimited manifestations of Him.

Another example of widening your perception is angels. You are probably aware of angels present in the room. But you cannot see them because they are in an expanded form—yet you can sense them. When you are in the glory zone, angels are there too, but in an expanded form. Sometimes they will contract and you will be able to see them in solid form. In fact, when you are in the presence and glory of God, the molecular structure of your own body starts to change. As mentioned in the previous chapter, you may arrive at a meeting very tired, but as you worship God you become energized physically, and even sickness departs. Your body, which is made of glory, comes in contact with a greater glory when worshiping or praying, and it changes your body's cellular structure. You start to feel lighter in the presence of God, as gravity seems to have less hold. At times, you may feel so light that you will fly away, because your body is changing into an expanded form.

Evangelist and healer Smith Wigglesworth, known for unusual miracles, has been quoted as saying, "The life that is in me is a thousand times bigger than I am outside."[1] As your spirit starts to expand, it affects your body. In fact, I believe that a person can get so light when the spirit expands in the glory that someone can be transported from one place to another!

Ezekiel was in the Spirit when he was transported to a valley of dry bones (see Ezek. 37:1.) Philip was transported after sharing the Scriptures with and baptizing the Ethiopian eunuch (see Acts 8:39-40). Elijah was often transported and would disappear for days and be found on a mountain somewhere far away. How is this possible? These experiences almost sound like a line from the "Star Trek" television program—"Beam me up, Scotty." But this is not as far-fetched as you may think. In the television show, you see a person standing in the "transporter," and when the right levers are pulled, the person's molecules and particles expand and travel to a different location. Then the makeup of the person retracts and re-concentrates, and the person arrives in one piece at the desired location.

When you are in the *glory zone* you feel light, and the very cells and molecules of your body change as your spirit begins to expand. I have had this happen to me several times. One time I was driving to a meeting between Paris, France, and Belgium. While still in Paris, my car broke down. I prayed for a miracle as the car was being towed. The mechanic said the engine was beyond repair. As I prayed, God miraculously repaired the car—to the surprise of the mechanic. By 7:30 P.M. I was back on the road but I had lost many hours of travel time. The meeting in Belgium started at 7 p.m., so I was already 30 minutes late and I still had a three-hour drive ahead in Friday night traffic. I called the pastor to tell him I would not make it in time to preach.

As I drove along, I decided to enjoy God's presence and worshiped Him without a care in the world. Then the Lord spoke to me and told me I would indeed arrive in time to preach. I had a hard time believing this so I just said, "Amen." I felt so light and full of glory while I was worshiping in my car, when 45 minutes into the drive I suddenly noticed I was already in Belgium, and the next exit was the one leading to the church. I was shocked because I never even saw the sign welcoming me to Belgium, let alone the very exit leading to the church. I pulled into the church parking lot at 8:15 p.m. and they were still worshiping, singing the last song. The pastor was very surprised to see me—it was impossible to make the trip in 45 minutes. The meeting was awesome! This has happened to us several times in different places and countries. I believe that being transported will become more common during this *Glory Invasion*.

WALKING THROUGH WALLS AND ON WATER

When you are experiencing extreme glory you are, in essence, in an expanded glory where the cellular structure of your body may expand. Jesus went through a lot— He come to earth as a man from an extreme *glory zone*—the throne of God. He was crucified, resurrected, glorified, took the keys of death, hell, and the grave, appeared to many witnesses, and ascended to the Father. Before He ascended, His body was still in its expanded form to such a degree that He could travel through walls after His resurrection, such as when He appeared to the disciples in the house without going through the front door—just as angels can, since they are permanently in the glory spirit realm. (See

Acts 1:10-11; Mark 16:1-7.) The molecules in your body are stretched out when in expanded form and will have no trouble going through walls at a certain level of high glory. Your spirit body basically dominates your physical body.

Just as sounds can travel through walls, you can travel through walls too, because you are made of sound and glory. When you are in an extreme state of glory, the sound waves of your body can penetrate walls as they expand. Even though you are a physical being made of sound *and* solid matter, you can still experience this phenomenon. Just as a television picture, which can travel thousands of miles from a satellite in space into your home and deliver sounds and light in the form of a picture, you are created from the same stuff—sound waves and light. Once the glory hits a certain level, it affects the sound waves inside your body and the entire molecular structure of your being.

Albert Einstein theorized that a fourth dimension exists where time is absent and eternity reigns. The fourth dimension that is beyond time and space can only be pierced by an object traveling at twice the speed of light. I believe Einstein was alluding to something he did not realize—the invisible Kingdom of Heaven that is all around us. As we are in the *glory zone*, we pierce through our current three-dimensional realm into another realm—the Kingdom of Heaven that is more real than what we see. If a scientist basing all his information on facts can realize there is another realm, how much easier should it be for us to believe? After all, there are examples of this other realm throughout the Scriptures.

How did Jesus and Peter walk on water? (See Matthew 14:22-33.) Jesus, who came in the form of a human like you and me, knew how to get into the glory realm, just as you and I can. The gravity and molecular structure of His body changed and He became light enough in the glory to walk across the surface of the water. It is possible that in His presence the molecular structure of the water could have changed and contracted tighter under each step He took, just as water can change into ice, a more solid form of the same substance. Jesus and Peter defied this world's three-dimensional law of gravity and operated out of Heaven's fourth or unlimited dimension as they both experienced the *glory zone*. By faith, Peter asked for permission to join Jesus as He walked on the water. Peter lunged into the glory realm where his body weight did not make him sink, but the water actually became solid enough for him to walk on. He was supported by the knowledge of his spirit and not his intellect. Likewise, Israel walked through the Red Sea, as God defied the laws of gravity by suspending the massive amounts of water in the air until His people traveled safely to the other side.

Walk by the spirit, not the flesh (see Gal. 5:16). The flesh is your natural, carnal, worldly, and three-dimensional limited way of thinking. As soon as Peter began to analyze and revert to past experience and acquired knowledge, he began to sink. I believe that although he did not understand how he was walking on water, he simply did it by faith. Faith with action will get you into the glory realm of creative miracles faster than anything else—even if you don't understand it. I hope that the insights in this book will give you some understanding of miracles and add to your faith and confidence about what goes on behind the scenes when these things occur.

GRAVITY-DEFYING MIRACLES

Saint Luke the Younger (A.D. 946) was a Greek believer who loved God and gave much to help the poor. He is one of the first saints recorded to have been seen levitating during prayer. Even after the seventeeth century and well into the Colonial Era these occurrences were recorded. Saint Joseph of Cupertino (1603–1663) was also known for levitating—he was often referred to as the "flying friar." His experiences are some of the best documented in church history. He was always in the Spirit and seemed oblivious and unshaken by anything in the natural world. He was not accepted into the Franciscan order because they considered him *too* focused on God. He was sent from one monastery to another, and finally they allowed him to become a priest at the age of 25.

It is recorded that Saint Joseph of Cupertino had extensive visions and heavenly trances triggered by simple things like music and hearing the name of Jesus. There are more than 70 recorded instances of Joseph levitating, along with numerous miraculous healings that were "not paralleled in the reasonably authenticated life of any other saint," according to the book, *Butler's Lives of the Saints*. Joseph's most radical instance of flight was when a group of monks were trying to place a large cross on the top of a church building. The cross was 36 feet high, taking the efforts of ten men to lift; when suddenly, Joseph flew 70 yards, picked it up "as if it were straw," and put it in place. Such phenomena kept Joseph's leaders from allowing him to celebrate mass in public for 35 years. They usually confined him to his room with a private chapel.

During a revival we held in Paris, France, in 1998 that lasted six months, we witnessed levitations, or people being lifted up off the ground. During the first weekend of meetings, the glory came so strong that I could not even grab the microphone to speak. People suddenly started to wail and weep for souls, and a 15-year-old girl in the back of the room slipped into deep travail and intercession for souls. While she was weeping, she was suddenly lifted five inches off the ground and then she flipped over in the air for a few more seconds, and then slowly came down. Her movements totally surprised some of the people seated near her who were attending the meeting simply out of curiosity. Immediately after the girl returned to her seat, 13 people ran up to be saved—each one had had suicidal tendencies.

These experiences were later recorded in a revival e-mail that was distributed throughout the United States and Canada. After this first weekend of revival meetings in Paris, for the next six months, four nights a week, souls were saved in each and every meeting, along with miracles, signs, and wonders displayed; and believers repented of sin in their lives. This revival was one of the highlights of our ministry work in that country, one of many places on the earth where we have seen God move in new ways.

The Scriptures say that Jesus' disciples watched as He ascended to Heaven (see Acts 1:9). Elijah was taken up in a chariot of fire (see 2 Kings 2:11). Today, there have been reports from various countries, including Argentina, about people levitating while preaching. If people involved in magic and sorcery can levitate and can draw a crowd in broad daylight, as has been known to happen in New York City by modern-day magicians and those using demonic power, how much more can the true children of God, blood-bought believers, move in even greater demonstrations of His power?

Again, it is not the miracle or act that is good or evil but rather the *source* of the miracle or act that is important. As long as it's Jesus and the power of Heaven in you, enjoy the journey and have a safe flight. God can use all things for His glory.

I truly believe that these examples from the Bible and recent history are foreshadows and glimpses of what the last day church will look like and do for His glory and to display His power. Many seekers are now being seduced by demonic power camouflaged as pure and innocent as they are searching for the supernatural. Will we rise up to the occasion as Moses did with his rod to challenge the current power and demonstrate an even greater power? Or will the followers of Jesus shy away from the challenge and play it safe behind church walls every Sunday? Some consider New Age followers to be the largest unreached people group in America and, along with Islam, the number of followers is growing in many nations worldwide.

Even powerful sorcerers in the Bible like Simon and Bar-Jesus were totally stunned and defeated by the superiority of the power of God demonstrated by the apostles and believers. Today, though, most Christians shy away from believing God's power and label it all as strange or dangerous. I believe that if the church doesn't begin to move in even greater power than is recorded in church history, we will lose the current generation that is starved to see the supernatural; millions flock to movies such as *Harry Potter* and join the demonically influenced streams and cults. We must rise up and lead them to the one true God of all power and love.

SOUNDS OF TRIUMPH

The walls of Jericho crumbled because people shouted—another amazing defiance of the law of gravity. What made the walls fall? The Israelites were told not to speak for one week. In this way they were conserving the power of the sound in their voices so on the day they released it their shouts would have greater power. Words and sound contain certain levels of energy. If you say "In the name of Jesus" with a tired voice, after having talked all day about nonsense, the power of your words is weakened. On the other hand, if you spend the day meditating on God and then speak, there is power in your words.

Imagine the Israelites spending an entire week not talking or being distracted or speaking negative words. The entire time their minds and spirits were preoccupied with God and with the anticipation of what He would do next. Then finally, after conserving all their sound waves, on His command, they together released one big shout and shofar blast—the power was like a sonic boom. Sounds waves full of glory and power like a laser were concentrated on the walls around the city of Jericho—and down they came.

I believe the walls were overpowered by the stream of concentrated sound waves emanating from the people's shouts, which blew out all the sound waves in the rocks. Because the rock wall was essentially made of the building block of sound and it was bombarded with greater sound waves of glory coming from an army of God's people, the wall crumbled as the very element that held it up was shattered. It is well known that if a person sings at a very high pitch long enough, glass will break—especially a fine crystal goblet. The sound pierces right through the glass, which is also made of sounds, and shatters it. A jet aircraft traveling faster than the speed of sound causes things on earth to shake because of the great power of the sound waves.

In November 2005, a cruise ship was attacked by pirates in the waters near Somalia. The ship's crew used a newly developed non-lethal weapon that sends out high-powered air vibrations. They aimed a sonic sound boom at the pirates who were trying to board the ship, and the blast knocked them off their feet. Fortunately, the cruise ship outmaneuvered the pirates and moved out into deeper waters.[2]

Can you imagine sounds loaded with the glory and power of God? There is a sound of God's glory that is released when we shout to the Lord corporately. As mentioned previously, sound is also energy and matter and it has energy and weight to it. Sound is a non-visible element but a very real object that, when in a concentrated form and filled with His glory, is a force to be reckoned with.

END-TIME SUPERHEROES

I grew up watching Superman and other superheroes on television. Superman could fly to another country or city in seconds, had x-ray vision, and performed superhuman feats of strength. The Invisible Girl could make herself disappear to get into or out of different situations. Flash Gordon could run faster than the eye could see. The Spiderman story was released as a movie and there is a resurgence of comic book heroes today as well. This is not an acceptance of such entertainment, but these are examples of the hunger people have for these types of supernatural experiences.

Maybe these characters were inspired by biblical heroes. After all, Samson lifted the gates of an entire city. He killed thousands of men with the jawbone of a donkey as well as many other amazing feats. Elijah outran a chariot, and Philip was transported faster than a blink to another town to preach. Jesus demonstrated the first invisible cloaking device when He disappeared from the midst of a crowd ready to stone Him! They had rocks in their hands and were looking right at Jesus—the next moment, He was gone. (See Judges 16:3; First Kings 18:44-46; Acts 8:39-40; John 8:59; 10:39.)

Superhuman strength and power come from a supernatural God. The kind of things that happened from Genesis through Revelation can and will happen again. I believe that God is now releasing supernatural visions and accurate, detailed words of knowledge about things happening behind closed doors that are baffling unbelievers. God is equipping superheroes for Jesus who will heal the sick and even resurrect the dead. They will take down demonic evil ones threatening cities and countries. The world is desperate for some Glory Superheroes for Jesus. While we wait for His return we can demonstrate His power of love and redemption.

Jesus is the true Superhero—and through the Holy Spirit, He is living inside of us. We have the ability to demonstrate His ultimate supernatural power. I believe that raising the dead, casting out demons, interpreting dreams, reading people's hearts, and being transported to help someone in need are just a few of the ways we can operate in the glory realm. People want superheroes and we can provide the Ultimate Superhero for them—God Almighty.

God provides supernatural experiences to those who are obedient. I have heard many testimonies about people who smuggle Bibles into Communist countries where Bibles are forbidden. Often, as these brave individuals approach security checkpoints, they pass directly through without even having to show their passports. God can easily expand the molecules in your body in such a glory that you become invisible.

ENDNOTES

1   Smith Wigglesworth, *Ever Increasing Faith* (New Kensington, PA: Whitaker House, 2001).

2.   Tom Walker, "Cruise Ship Attacked by Pirates," *The Sunday Times—Great Britain.* http://www.timesonline.co.uk/article/0,2087-1859626,00.html (accessed November 2, 2006).

CHAPTER THREE
REVELATORY REALMS AND PORTALS

Genesis 28:10-12 speaks of Jacob's *"ladder…set up on the earth, and its top reached to heaven; and there the angels of God were ascending and descending on it."* In Second Corinthians 12:2, Paul talks about the third heaven. There are also many testimonies and current experiences of God's modern-day apostles, prophets, and believers that refer to revelatory realms and heavenly portals.

I had an encounter of this type in Israel. As we drove into Bethel in our bulletproof bus (which we were required to rent), we were hoping to find the spot where Jacob's ladder was located. There were no signs indicating the location, so our bus driver took us to a settlement and told us to pray there, as he was tired of the search. We walked into the woods and there found a large slab of concrete next to some ruins.

We began to pray and worship the Lord and then we simply lay down and soaked in the presence of God while our worship leader played music for the next few hours. During this time something unusual happened. People on our team, comprising people from the United States, Europe, and the South Pacific islands, were taken to the third heaven. After the experience, they reported seeing other team members in Heaven and all related having the same conversations.

Team members reported having been taken in the Spirit to the streets of gold and other parts of Heaven. It was amazing to hear the people, interviewed separately, tell of their experiences, and how they saw other team members in Heaven, and their almost identical descriptions of what they saw there. Their similar recollections confirmed their validity and credibility. Three people from our team (including my wife) who were from three different continents said they were transported over the earth and Western Europe. All three saw the same cities in Europe on fire burning. They related seeing this vision only months before the car-burning riots in Paris and the London bombings in 2005. The Lord put a burden on them to begin to intercede for the souls that could be saved, revealing that some level of catastrophic destruction was coming and to pray to lessen or avert it. Three people taken in the Spirit to the same cities to pray for the same things in the same experience makes us realize how real this realm is.

Since that time, many people in our meetings have had third heaven experiences. The apostle Paul writes about a man who went to the third heaven—most believe he was talking about his own experience. Both Elijah and Enoch took a one-way trip to Heaven, both in body and spirit.

While in the most remote parts of French Guiana, a pastor and I were talking about the meeting we had just finished and about the witch doctors, sorcerers, and gang members who had just been saved with signs and wonders following. It was after midnight, and as we shared, I saw an angel on the pastor's back for over 30 minutes. I told him about the angel and he was stunned, and said his back had been burning for the past 30 minutes.

Just then we both saw a ladder going up to the sky and angels ascending and descending from it. We saw angels coming and going until about 3 A.M. All the barn animals outside were making a lot of noise, as they could sense what was happening. We both received direct impartation and instruction from Heaven about the next five to ten years of our life and ministry, much of which has already unfolded just from that one experience.

Visitations, dreams, visions, and heavenly experiences are of great worth. They can alter and accelerate years of your life and ministry because of one heavenly encounter. Mary was changed with one angelic visit, as were Moses, Joshua, David, Elizabeth, and many more.

Just as you can be transported over the earth because of the glory, you can also be transported upward to Heaven. Your spirit, and at times your spirit and body together, can be taken there. The apostle Paul could not tell if his spirit only or both his body and spirit were taken to the third heaven to see things, many of which he was not allowed to describe (see 2 Cor. 12:4). In the *glory zone* there is no distance between time and space, Heaven or earth. The same way you can be taken horizontally from one city to another, you can be taken vertically from earth to Heaven.

DREAMS, VISIONS, AND TRANCES

In these last days I believe God is choosing to use dreams and visions as major means of speaking to His people and giving direction and answers to prayer.

Dreams and visions differ. Dreams are usually more prophetic and symbolic, not usually literal. Visions are actual pictures of what will happen. Though dreams take more experience and maturity to interpret than visions, they often offer much more detail once interpreted. That is why it says in the Bible that *"old men shall dream dreams, and your young men shall see visions"* (Joel 2:28). It may take more maturity to understand dreams than visions—a picture can say a thousand words.

For instance, Peter had a dream about eating all the unclean animals (see Acts 10:9-15). It was in no way a literal dream. God was not telling him to go to an "all you can eat" pork and shrimp buffet. Peter was even surprised about the dream and told God that he had never eaten animals considered unclean. Actually the dream was speaking metaphorically about bringing the Gospel to the Gentiles, who were considered unclean by the Jews of that day. In fact, they were forbidden to even enter the home of a Gentile. Therefore, Peter's dream was revolutionary and symbolic, not a new doctrine about what Jews could eat. For the first time he was to share the Gospel with the Gentiles. The proper interpretation of the dream changed the entire course of the Church, resulting in Cornelius becoming the first Gentile convert. (See Acts 10:17-48.)

How can you experience dreams, visions, and third heaven encounters? One thing I have noticed is that many people receive visions and dreams while sleeping, daydreaming, or soaking in the spirit—all are in a relaxed state. Often upon awakening I hear the voice of God or receive a vision. Why do people receive better when they are resting or sleeping? When you are resting, your mind is relaxed and able to receive from Heaven. When your mind is so full of the cares of life, when God tries to speak to you, you unknowingly block it out because the "mailbox is full." When you are praying but fully awake, often it is still hard to see a vision or hear the voice of God because your mind is prayerfully active with many thoughts and concerns.

One way to receive revelation, visions, and dreams while awake is to lie down while listening to soft worship music and simply relax your mind and body—not praying out loud but soaking up the music and presence of God. Then see what images pop into your mind and spirit and go with them. Oftentimes God speaks when we are still. Also, before going to sleep you can ask God to give you a dream, and He will often grant your request because you are asking in faith. I notice that I receive more dreams when I ask Him for them than when I don't. Ask and you shall receive. I also ask Him for visions while I am praying or soaking in His presence.

PRACTICING VISIONS

You can also practice receiving visions. For example, one day while driving two hours to a meeting in Miami, Florida, I received a vision of some of the healings that would take place later that night. You may receive visions while driving because of the monotony of driving without distractions. While in that mode I could see a man being healed of a cataract. Then the Lord told me to look further and see what other details of the man I could see. As I looked again at the vision, I started to make out the face of the man. He looked about 50 years old, so I jotted that down. Then I saw a second vision of a Hispanic-looking lady, her age, and her sickness. When I arrived at the meeting I looked around to see if I could find the people in the crowd. Sure enough, the man I saw was there and so was the lady.

As I was invited to speak, I pointed to the man and asked him if he had cataracts. In shock, he nodded his head. Then I called him up and asked him if he was around 50 years old. He answered into the microphone that he was exactly 50 years old. This totally exploded the faith level in the room. When I spoke to the Hispanic girl and asked her to confirm the sickness and her age as I knew them to be from the vision. She said I was accurate, and the audience was amazed. As you can imagine, the remainder of the meeting was blessed with more such miracles and an awesome presence of God.

Basically we can all receive visions. They are simply pictures in your mind that God is bringing to you. Visions are not always accompanied with goose bumps, an angel, or an audible voice. More often than not it's a mental picture God gives you and you simply go with what you are seeing. *Seeing* is the essence of a vision. Start to practice receiving visions and write down the mental picture you receive when you are praying, soaking, driving, or whenever you experience one. Then compare notes and see which ones are accurate and begin to hone the gift for His glory.

Trances are similar to visions or dreams but occur while you are in a sleeplike state. Often people call them daydreams. Some have been known to slip into a trance while driving and then wonder how they were able to drive and be lost in the trance at the same time.

GEOGRAPHICAL PORTALS TO HEAVEN

There are some places on earth that already have an open portal to Heaven, which makes it easier to receive revelation. For instance, when you are in a church or city that is experiencing revival, there is an open portal allowing a greater awareness of the supernatural—possibly a Jacob's ladder-type of portal with angels ascending and descending. The biggest portal is in Jerusalem. I believe it is the easiest place to hear from God, and receive dreams and visions; angelic appearances are also common occurrences there.

Of all the cities in the world, He has designated Jerusalem as the city of the great King. (See Matthew 5:35.) It is the largest open-Heaven portal on earth—not to mention the fact that Jesus died, was buried, and rose from the dead there and will return there; and the first major revivals in the Book of Acts also took place in Jerusalem.

Also, almost every major religion has a presence in Jerusalem because they value the portal even if they do not know the Messiah. Many battles throughout history have been fought in and for this city. Bethel is another city in Israel where we easily received visions and third heaven encounters because Jacob already opened it. Once a portal has been opened I believe there is a permanent door in that place allowing it to be reopened much more easily because someone already paved the way.

Genesis 28:17 says, *"This is the gate of heaven"* speaking about Jacob's ladder located in the city of Bethel. Jacob did not say that it *was* the gate, but that it *is* the gate, or a doorway of Heaven.

Other portals are found in more infamous cities. Sedona, Arizona, is one such portal—currently known as the largest New Age town in the Southwest. It has also been named the most beautiful town in America by *USA Today*, as it is surrounded by breathtaking red, Rocky Mountains, and was once the main site for filming many of the early television westerns. I have found that when you pray and enter into the Spirit in Sedona, there is a huge wave of God's glory there and clarity in hearing God's voice that is unlike many other places. Why and how is this so? Even though you can obviously see the New Age influence and many cults are headquartered there—great glory also resides there: great darkness and great light. Often, the greater the darkness, the greater is the light and destiny over a city.

The Native Americans called Sedona a sacred town. Legend reveals that they considered Sedona so sacred that at one time they would only let chiefs or medicine men (witch doctors) in to pray. Greater Sedona later became a meeting place for Indians from all over the Southwest. When rival tribes met and migrated to Sedona, they ceased fighting and would worship and practice their religions. The Native Americans have regarded Sedona's environs as sacred and special, long before the settlers arrived.[1]

I believe the Native Americans could sense the glory of God in this town and did not know how to respond, as they had not yet heard the Gospel. And so they worshiped what they knew. They could sense the open heavenly portal. To this day thousands of tourists each year travel to Sedona to get a spiritual high, not knowing why they are drawn to the city. We are seeing God now reveal Himself there to those who are true seekers of the true Creator.

In the early 1900s, Sedona was a place where Christians from all over the United States gathered to hold large conferences and retreats as God's glory filled the city—long before it was claimed as a New Age vortex city. God has already designated Sedona as an open portal, a high place over the Southwest. He is waiting for His people to completely take it back, crack open the portal even wider, and invite the world to soak in God's presence as they enter the city limits and find the King of Glory. I believe that after this occurs, there will be a domino effect over the entire Western part of the United States, especially the areas of the Rocky Mountain chain all the way from Arizona up to the Northwest and into Western Canada, where the New Age movement is the most concentrated.

High up in the Himalaya Mountains in Tibet, the highest point on the earth, there are rumors that great evil is lurking there. It seems that both the Lord and the enemy like to dominate the high places—which are often mountainous. The Bible talks about the Lord dwelling on Mount Zion in Jerusalem and of coming up to meet the Lord at the mountain of the Lord (see Ps. 76:2; 68:16; Isa. 2:3). Many passages talk about heavenly visitations in high mountainous places like the Mount of Transfiguration (see Matt. 17:1-3); Mount Sinai, where Moses climbed to meet God (see Exod. 34:2,5); and Mount Carmel, where Elijah confronted the false prophets and the priests of Baal (see 1 Kings 18:19-20).

Supernatural powers from satan and God on the earth seem to focus on mountains and high places. I believe that Tibet's highest mountain range is a place that God has ordained to demonstrate His beauty and majesty and a place to meet with God in a special way, as it is physically the closest point between Heaven and earth. Satan seems to dominate that region, but why? One reason is because there is already a natural portal of glory there, making it easier for Tibetan

Buddhist monks to access the supernatural. But they are only accessing the second heavens where demons and principalities dwell. After God gets hold of that area, it will be an entire open "Heaven on earth" atmosphere once again.

Satan tries to entrench himself in areas called to be great portals to keep them closed up and inaccessible to us. I believe that even Mecca in Saudi Arabia was once a portal of glory, because people are drawn there to worship and to experience spirituality. They may not worship our Messiah but they feel the urge to worship. Mecca is a portal; but again, it is being used to access the second heaven only. This is where dark principalities dwell, but it will one day be redeemed and the purpose for which God caused people to be drawn there will be revealed.

ENDNOTE

1. Kate Ruland-Thorne, *Sedona's Legends and Legacies* (Phoenix, AZ: Primer Publishers, 1989).

CHAPTER FOUR

PROPHETIC GLORY

As it was in the days of Elijah, so will it be in the coming days. God is raising up modern-day Elijahs around the world to overcome the kingdom of darkness and bring in the Kingdom of God through an invasion of *prophetic glory*.

The most common manifestation of the glory of God in Elijah's life was his prophetic gifts intertwined with the glory. Many people today are majoring in the prophetic gift but not in the glory. You can have a prophetic gifting flow at times even when you are not necessarily in the glory. God's gifts are irrevocable but they do not always operate in the glory realm.

The same goes for those with a healing anointing. Just because there are healings, prophecies, or gifts in operation does not mean that the glory of God is present. Some in the last days will even say, *"Lord, Lord, have we not prophesied in Your name, cast out demons in Your name, and done many wonders in Your name?"* The Lord's response was: *"I never knew you"* (Matt. 7:22-23).

If you put the primary emphasis on the glory, which only comes through intimacy with Him, plus a close relationship, and times of waiting on the Lord, then when you do prophesy, the prophecy will be earth-shaking and change entire nations. When King Saul was on his way to try to kill David, he ran into the company of prophets and prophesied all day instead of pursuing David (see 1 Sam. 10:10-11). This does not mean that he impacted many people while he prophesied.

Although your prophecy may be accurate, the weight of the effect of your prophecy will depend on the level of the glory and presence of God in your life. Two people can give the exact same prophecy and witness different results. One can give it in the glory and see immediate and drastic life-changing results, while the other with the same word, running on his gift alone and not the glory, will not see the same results.

We can't use the gift without the Giver. That is why I call it *prophetic glory*. The same is true when you use your prophetic gift in words of knowledge for healings and miracles. Make sure the glory of God is present; then give those same words, and there will be many instant miracles. If you give the words before the right time and the glory of God has not fully come, the words, though true, usually will not have the same immediate and God-glorifying results. This was the secret of Elijah and Elisha. They knew the Spirit of God, and when the glory was present and when it was not.

A few examples: I was being interviewed in Phoenix, Arizona, on TBN, a Christian television station. While on the air, the glory of God hit me strongly. I began to prophesy, mentioned someone's full name and said that person needed to come to the meetings we were holding in that city and to give his life back to God. I understood, through the glory, that this person had been in the ministry but had fallen away, and that God was going to pick him back up. Sure enough, the next night the man came to our meetings because he heard his first and last name on television—his life changed dramatically.

Another time, I was ministering in Hammond, Louisiana, and again a man's entire name, first and last name, was given to me when the glory fell. The only problem: no one claimed to be that man. A woman finally came up and said that it was her husband's name but that he was not at the meeting, but was at home. Now even though the man was not present, I could still minister to him directly while the glory was present. Although in the glory there is no distance of time or space, if I waited until after the glory left, I would not be able to pray for this man in the same way. So I declared over his wife, "In the name of Jesus, come back!"—speaking to the husband who was not present.

I did not understand why I was saying this over him, since he was not even in the meeting, but I was simply obeying the leading of the Holy Spirit. The next day the woman returned and testified. She explained that her husband had been in a coma for many days. The moment I called out his name, he came out of the coma. When she had gone home that night after the prophecy, he was awake and eating, which he had not done in a long time. The greater the glory that is present, the greater the effect of the prophetic word. It's one thing to learn how to receive prophetic words and to hear His voice, but it's quite another to know when to give the prophecy and to discern when the glory is present.

Jesus moved in this realm often. He prophetically declared to a fig tree that it would die. At that moment it started to die, and the next time He saw the tree, death was all over it! (See Mark 11:12-14,20-24.) I believe that prophecy as we now know it will start to change. Prophecy will no longer be about a future event waiting to come to pass. As the prophetic words are coming out of our mouths, that which we say will be already created and in motion before we finish speaking. Why? Because in the glory realm there is no time. When you speak from the glory realm you are actually allowing God to create that which you are speaking. It is the same principle that God used in Genesis when He had the Spirit hovering, and then He spoke. It would behoove us to concentrate more on the glory realm as our first priority rather than on our gifts.

The apostle Paul had a prophetic vision in the glory about how to avoid the loss of life on his soon-to-be shipwreck. Even though he was a prisoner, it did not hinder him from tapping into God's power and the prophetic glory. (See Acts 27.)

GREATER GLORY

The greater the glory, the quicker things will happen. Jesus prophesied that the centurion's servant would be healed and that very hour he was healed. (See Matthew 8:5-10.) Mary had received a prophecy from the angel of the Lord that she would be pregnant with Jesus. (See Luke 1:26-38.) This was a glory-filled event—an angelic visitation coming fresh from the throne of God. How long do you think it took for that prophecy to come to pass? Instantly! She was already pregnant afterward because in the next verse she is hastily walking over to visit Elizabeth, and the baby John the Baptist leaped in his mother's womb at the presence of Jesus in Mary (see Luke 1:39-45). This event took place at the most three days later (or however long it took to walk to Elizabeth's house) after the angelic visitation and prophecy! Conception was immediate at the moment the prophecy was given, for the Holy Spirit hovered over her (see verse 35) just as in Genesis when the Spirit hovered over the waters at Creation.

> *Then Mary said, "Behold the maidservant of the Lord! Let it be to me according to your word." And the angel departed from her. Now Mary arose in those days and went into the hill country with haste, to a city of Judah, and entered the house of Zacharias and greeted Elizabeth. And it happened, when Elizabeth heard the greeting of Mary, that the babe leaped in her womb; and Elizabeth was filled with the Holy Spirit. Then she spoke out with a loud voice and said, "Blessed are you among women, and blessed is the fruit of your womb! But why is this granted to me, that the mother of my Lord should come to me? For indeed, as soon as the voice of your greeting sounded in my ears, the babe leaped in my womb for joy"* (Luke 1:38-44).

After a glory-filled prophecy is given, the only thing to do is to believe it. That is very important and should not be neglected. The greater the glory is the greater the miracles will be but also the greater the judgment. Swift miracles will happen, but also swift correction or judgment. Both will accelerate as the glory is accelerated, depending on our response.

Zacharias received the same kind of glorious prophetic word from an angel. The only difference: he doubted the prophecy. He received a second prophecy saying that he would become mute. It happened quickly—he become mute. The baby John was quickly conceived. All had happened quickly because the prophecies were in the glory when the Spirit was moving. Why did God have to make Zacharias mute? Because the same power that is released through the spoken prophetic word in the glory can bring life or death. Zacharias had the power to kill the prophecy in the same way it had come to life—by speaking in unbelief while in the glory and allowing the opposite to occur; he thus nearly created a disaster by negative declarations in the glory. In order to stop this from happening, God had to take away his words by allowing him to be mute so he would not undo the prophetic declaration or prophesy the wrong thing. (See Luke 1:11-22.) When the glory is present, there is great power in our words, and often our words are prophetic, whether we realize it or not.

Paul had a similar experience. He was trying to convert the Roman leader of Cyprus, but a sorcerer was hindering his efforts. Paul in the spirit realm was warring with the demonic power so it would not prevent the proconsul leader's salvation. Finally in the Spirit of God's glory, Paul used a great weapon that dealt a blow to this sorcerer—the weapon of prophetic glory. Under the leading of the Holy Spirit, Paul prophesied that he would become blind. Instantly the sorcerer went blind for days, and Paul was able to lead the proconsul to the Lord without distraction. With great power comes great responsibility. Paul used the gifts wisely in simple obedience. These kinds of demonstrations are rare in the sense that the prophetic was used to bring blindness, as the proconsul's salvation was very important to God and to the island nation. (See Acts 13:1-12.)

When Peter prophesied to Ananias and Sapphira, the glory of God was growing. The people had just experienced a second Pentecost, and many people were being healed. Multitudes were joining the apostles, and His glory was everywhere. People even gave their homes and lands to the Lord. But not Ananias and Sapphira. They were not honest about what they claimed they gave. Because of their deception, Peter prophetically declared that they would die. After he questioned Ananias, and he was untruthful, instantly he died. Then, when Sapphira arrived, Peter prophesied her death and instantly she died (see Acts 5:1-12).

This is a very striking passage, which many people have a hard time comprehending. Why was this sin so harshly and swiftly judged when surely there were greater sins being committed in the New Testament church? Why were the people who mocked those speaking in new tongues at Pentecost not judged as harshly? Because the glory in Acts 5 was considerably greater and had increased since the events recorded in Acts 2. This Acts 5 revival was on a greater level, as He was taking the Church from glory to glory. The apostles were not just laying hands on the sick anymore. Now Peter's shadow alone was healing the sick.

Because the glory had gone to a greater level, so did the prophetic gift and the swiftness of its fulfillment. Also, I believe that God did not want this new move of His to be hindered by sin. Ananias and Sapphira lied with the spoken word, the same principle, but in reverse, and they did so while the glory was present. That which we speak while in the glory is very important. The next time the glory comes in a meeting, be careful of careless words or of creating something with words that God did not intend. Honor the King of glory.

Because the glory is currently a popular subject, there is a danger for those who pretend to be in the glory to gather a crowd. I believe that a new chapter of the glory, *judgment glory*, may be on the horizon— just as it was with Ananias and Sapphira. God is not fooling around in these last days and He won't allow people to counterfeit what He really wants to do.

STEPPING INTO NEW REALMS

One night while I was preaching at Ruth Heflin's campground in Ashland, Virginia, I had secretly asked God to increase the prophetic gift on my life through Ruth Heflin's prophetic mantle during the day meetings. I even approached her to sow an offering into her life, asking God for a return with an increase of the prophetic gift that was on her. After all, she had a prophetic gift that opened doors to impact nations, presidents, and kings. During the evening service while I was preaching, the Lord told me to prophesy over Ruth Heflin! I was shocked; but I pointed to Ruth, who was sitting on the stage, and prophesied while the glory was present.

I prophesied that although she had already met many presidents and world leaders she would soon be in a meeting with the pope of Rome! I said that her visit with the pope would cause a chain reaction, and that this would somehow trigger a major release of revival to millions of Catholics around the world who would be saved. Immediately afterward I was kicking myself for uttering such a crazy word. Ruth came to the microphone to confirm that this was indeed what she secretly had been praying about. She explained that two weeks before, God had even opened up a contact to help her meet the pope.

Shortly after I returned home from the camp meeting, I received an e-mail stating that Ruth Heflin was in Israel during the pope's visit to the Holy Land and that she was invited to a special meeting with the pope present. Prophetic glory changes things!

In the African nation of Gabon other miraculous things happened. While in the airplane heading to Gabon, the Lord instructed me to prophesy over the government of that nation and He said that the door would open. I declared this while in the air. When I arrived, the pastor asked me if there was anything he could do for me. I asked him for an audience with the president or vice president of the nation. Within days, I was in front of the country's vice president prophesying to him and his wife in his mansion. They both wept openly at the prophetic word they desperately needed to hear at that time in their lives. Two hours later, Pastor Yonggi Cho from South Korea arrived at their home to also speak a word to the vice president. He was in Gabon to hold a crusade but went first to the vice president to prophesy over him. Pastor Cho gave the same prophecy as I did—word for word! This was an important sign to the man in office and a great encouragement to me in the area of hearing from the Lord.

There is no limit in the glory. Once you are in the thick presence of His glory, simply say what He tells you to say. In the last experience I shared with you, I was not asked to prophesy in front of a crowd of people. I was alone on the airplane and as I prophesied, things had opened up on the ground by the time I arrived. Prophecy sends angels on your behalf to arrange these kinds of things.

The most recent experience I had was flying into Washington, D.C.. During the flight, the Lord told me that I would be inside the White House within the next few days praying for the nation at a very critical time. I could sense the unquestionable heavy weight of

God's glory at the time. As I was in the *glory zone,* I immediately declared that which was told to me—that the doors are open to the White House. In the natural I did not know anyone with such connections; but when I arrived, the pastor wanted to show me the White House; so, like most tourists, we drove by the outside of the impressive large building. Silently I began to prophesy a second time about going in. This all happened on a Friday.

Though I told no one about the prophecy, on Sunday morning a woman approached me and asked me if the Lord had told me to go into the White House to pray. I was stunned and said that it was true. The woman said she had a friend who worked in the Executive Office Building right next to the White House, where many of the White House staff work. She asked for my Social Security number and said that my records and history would have to be checked by security and the FBI—a process that can take months to complete. But this woman had also heard from the Lord that somehow I was to go in right away. Within 24 hours of giving her my Social Security number, and with the escort of the White House staff worker, I was cleared to go inside the White House and was given a private tour.

I prayed in each of the important rooms where many decisions are made on a daily basis—decisions affecting our nation and the world. It is so important to declare what God is telling you while the atmosphere of His glory is present. This happened a second time, only six months later, when my wife and I had the opportunity to pray and declare things prophetically in the West Wing, including the Oval Office, the Situation Room, the press corps area, and other key locations.

> So I prophesied as I was commanded; and as I prophesied, there was a noise, and suddenly a rattling; and the bones came together, bone to bone (Ezekiel 37:7).

As we see in this passage, the moment Ezekiel prophesied, the noise began, and the miracle started the moment the prophecy commenced. Prophecy does not just foretell; it creates that which is being said! It is the tool that brings it to pass. Confessing what you want

God to do is different from declaring what He is saying right now while the glory is present. Ezekiel continued to prophesy, and the miracles continued.

> *Also He said to me, "Prophesy to the breath, prophesy, son of man, and say to the breath, 'Thus says the Lord God: "Come from the four winds, O breath, and breathe on these slain, that they may live"'"* (Ezekiel 37:9).

You can imagine what happened next. Remember that it is not the prophetic gift alone that is so important, but the fact that Ezekiel is prophesying while the Spirit is moving and the glory of God is present—he was first in the Spirit of the Lord. (See Ezekiel 37:1.) He clearly explains that the Spirit of the Lord transported him to this place to prophesy. Here is what happened after the second prophecy.

> *So I prophesied as He commanded me, and breath came into them, and they lived, and stood upon their feet, an exceedingly great army* (Ezekiel 37:10).

Both Elijah and Elisha walked and lived in the prophetic glory realm, and when they spoke it caused Heaven and earth, kings and nations, to react and respond. The prophets of old have much to teach the present-day generation. They did whatever it took to get in a place with God for His glory to come so they could be effective. They knew that without His Presence nothing could happen. Jesus even said, *"I am the vine, you are the branches. He who abides in Me, and I in him, bears much fruit; for without Me you can do nothing"* (John 15:5).

Elijah and Elisha prophesied the opening of wombs, rain and drought, provisions, resurrections and deaths, and the list goes on. God is now raising up prophetic glory gifts so people can report terrorist plots to the police and help stop attacks before they happen. More and more, the police force, media, and governments will be depending on the new Elijahs, begging to know *the Word of the Lord* regarding their national safety and security. We owe it to our generation and the next to press into this end-time grace of prophetic glory for His purposes!

SECTION II

HARVEST AND GLORY

CHAPTER FIVE

REAPING GLORY

VIOLENT SOWING

In the Old Testament, Elijah and Elisha both moved in the area of miraculous provision; both were shadows of Jesus, who moved in provisional miracles.

> *May the Lord, the God of your father, increase you a thousand-fold more than you are and bless you, just as He has promised you!* (Deuteronomy 1:11 NASB)

In order to reap the great harvest, there will need to be a great harvest of resources and finances. God has already revealed many of these things, and they have been a great blessing to many ministries worldwide. But before we can walk into mighty reaping there must be violent sowing. When the widow gave Elijah her last meal, it was a violent attack against the poverty, fear, and reality of her present circumstances. (See First Kings 17:8-16.) Such leaps of faith cause great reaping to take place.

When you sow sacrificially into a ministry moving in the glory and blessing of the Lord, God causes the same measure given plus the measure of glory that rests on that ministry to be multiplied supernaturally. We have seen people receive even 1,000 times what they have given after we have prayed and blessed the gift sown into the anointing and glory operating in our ministry. The only time this happens is when a gift is sown sacrificially into good ground. The good ground is where the glory and presence of God is moving. It's the same fertile ground that Adam and Eve walked on—the glory of God with them in The Garden.

We see this same glory ground with the boy who gave Jesus all the food he had. With only a few loaves and fish sown into Jesus, the glory manifested, and God provided a miracle (see John 6:5-13). God took the sacrificial gift sown into good ground and fed over 5,000 people. God performed a thousandfold multiplication that day. All it took was a young boy willing to give it all for God's purposes. The Bible says to *receive the Kingdom of Heaven as a little child in order to enter into it* (see Luke 18:17). Too often we calculate what we think we should give after looking at the bills waiting to be paid and our checking and savings account balances—a child does not calculate, he just gives.

In the Old and New Testaments, whenever the glory of God appeared Israel often stopped and took up an offering to honor the God of glory. It was an automatic response to the glory that God required when His manifest presence and glory appeared not because He needs it, but because He knows that this is what man treasures the most—his gold, silver, and provision. It is one of the highest acts of worship to give up something for God's glory that is truly, personally costly. What may seem like a lot to one may be insignificant to another.

Jesus apparently was very interested in offerings, as He watched to see how much each person gave. He noticed that the poor widow gave more than all the wealthy people—she gave her last two mites, 100 percent of what she had. (See Mark 12:41-44.) It's the percentage of our sacrificial giving that determines whether or not it is sacrificial. This is not to say that everyone should always give all. But when the glory comes or God tells you to sow into a ministry or place where the glory is moving, giving generously into that which God is already blessing with His glory will cause the greatest return.

Generosity is determined by the percentage of what you have that you give, not the actual amount. Solomon gave 1,000 animals on the altar, and his sacrifice resulted in the heavens opening up and God granting Solomon everything he needed and whatever he desired (see 1 Kings 3:4-13). He did not squander God's benevolence—he asked for wisdom. Solomon's sacrificial gift was in accordance with what he already had, and great blessing followed.

Should we give only to receive? No, we give because it is the highest act of worship. But at the same time, you give knowing that you will also receive. It's not the only reason to give but it is one of the benefits. When you praise and worship God with songs, you do it out of love; yet you also believe for God's presence to come upon you in return. It is not selfish if your motives for receiving are good and for His glory. What farmer would go out sowing and then feel ashamed to reap what he has sown? This is how God created the order of things.

VIOLENT REAPING

The kingdom of heaven suffers violence, and the violent take it by force (Matthew 11:12b).

I got excited about this aspect of the glory, for not only did our ministry want to see spiritual manifestations of the glory, but we believed that there needed to be great material manifestations of glory as well. One translation for *glory* is "wealth." It is similar to when a king or queen arrives with all the fanfare, pomp and circumstance, glory, and wealth. I'm sure you have heard the phrase, "Here comes so-and-so walking down the street in all his glory."

One day God asked me if I wanted to sow into the glory so that the heavens would open up in a new way. I said, "Yes, Lord!" I began to study the Book of Acts and noticed how people gave sacrificially to their spiritual fathers, the apostles, and laid the profits from the sale of their homes and lands at their feet. I believe that for the *Elijah glory anointing* and the full apostolic mantle to fall upon the Church, there needs to be a great love for those we follow in the Lord. We need to trust them with even our material blessings for the furthering of the Gospel, and to honor the gift and glory of God in them.

During my Sunday morning message, God told me to give my car away to the local pastor of the church we attended at the time. I was shocked. I realized that this was not just another token gift, but that God wanted something more of me. As I was experiencing a new glory in my ministry, it needed to be accompanied by a new level of

71

sacrificial giving for God to trust us to walk in the higher realms of the Spirit and finances.

Our level of obedience in sacrificial giving is totally connected to the level of the supernatural and the miraculous that God will entrust to us. The Bible clearly points out in Luke 16:12 and Luke 19:17-26 that if God cannot trust us to give our material riches when He asks for it, He certainly will not trust us with great spiritual riches. This is one reason many are not seeing the extraordinary miracles, salvations, and provisions as experienced in the Book of Acts. Are we willing to free up ourselves in this area of finances to see God's power resurrected in our day?

In the middle of the Sunday morning service I gave the car away. At first, just thinking about it seemed hard. But then, as I realized God Himself had prompted me and that only a greater blessing from Heaven could come of it for both the pastor and myself, I then got excited about giving away our only car. When excitement accompanies giving beyond the norm, miracles are ahead. As I gave the car, the glory of God broke into the service, signs and wonders appeared, and many material miracles happened to the church. Many gave spontaneously, and almost violently. One of the miracles that followed: the landlord decided to give approximately $200,000 worth of repair work that the church building needed.

Several months later I began to question the Lord. *"Lord, we do need another car and I did give that other one away joyfully. Where is our next vehicle?"* The Lord told me that the moment I gave the car away in the glory, the car He had for us was ready—all I had to do was receive it by faith. This is an example of "violent reaping." The next week I was off to preach in Germany. When I arrived, I noticed a car dealership across the street from the church, so I visited the German car shop and looked at the fine cars. I picked out the car I believed we were to have and told God that before I left, if nothing else happened, I would drive away with this car by faith.

The last night of our conference in Germany a man came up to me that I had never met. He told me that he had a car for me. I received a car that night and drove it home—it was almost identical to the one in the shop! If I had not put myself into a "reaping mode" by physically going to look at cars, and had not attempted to prophetically walk into and receive my harvest, I may not have ever received that car or any car. This is simply training for greater advances of the Kingdom.

Many have preached on seedtime and sowing, but now God is releasing revelation about *how to reap the harvest*. The Bible talks about *the reapers and the harvest of the last days* (see Rev. 14:15-16). The prophet Amos said, *"The plowman shall overtake the reaper and the treader of grapes him who sows seed"* (Amos 9:13b). I purposely reaped that car because I went out looking for it. A farmer does not sit down to his dinner table waiting for the harvest to come jump onto his plate. After he has sown and the time to reap has come, he must go out looking for the harvest.

How many times have you given an offering and then weeks or months went by and you totally forgot about what you gave? You did not reap and you wondered why the harvest was taking so long. You thought that God would just give you whatever was due to you as He wills. How will you know if what you received was from your giving if you don't even remember what you gave?

The truth is, God is telling us to go reap. It's like sitting under an apple tree. An apple falls on your head and you say, "Wow, where did this come from? I am blessed today." Well, you maybe got blessed by accident or by grace, but for every apple that falls by accident, there is a whole tree to be reaped on purpose.

Start to reap on purpose the things God has promised you instead of receiving only what He spoon-feeds you. Start to look for the harvest. Violent reaping consists of sowing violently and abundantly, and then looking for the harvest, and reaping it abundantly on purpose. The next time you are blessed you won't be wondering, *"I wonder why I got blessed."* You will know because you were expecting it, as a farmer expects a harvest.

When God told Israel to walk into the Promised Land, they had to purposely and physically enter and take the land. God had already given it to them, but it was 40 years before they actually went in and reaped His promise. Likewise, God has promised and prophesied some things to you, and you may have even sown generously, believing for that thing to come to pass. Arise and take the first steps to possessing what is already laid up for you. Go and spy out the land, ministry, property, equipment—whatever God has already ripened for your picking. The act of looking by faith will begin to release the blessing.

Elijah told the widow to reap purposely by gathering as many bowls as she could so God could fill them. (See Second Kings 4:1-7.)

FAITH VERSUS HOPE

How many times have you asked God to bless a certain project, hoping that the money would come in? You probably hoped God would do it but you did not have full assurance that He would. There is a big difference between faith and hope. Faith is now; hope is future tense. If you hope for it, it's still out there in the future. When you know that you know it's done, it's a now thing. The reason for this is in the giving. Have you given in such a way that when it came time for you to reap you had sown enough to reap what you were trying to receive? This is why it is important to keep track or at least have an idea of what we have sown in the glory. Usually, when the giving requires a sacrifice, you can remember it well. When it comes time for you to purchase that property or go on a mission trip, you will know you have sown enough to reap it if God multiplies your giving. You will know if you have enough in your heavenly bank account to make a withdrawal and take a step of faith in that area.

If God multiplies what you gave by 30, 60, or 100, and it still does not add up to what you are believing for, you may want to wait and keep sowing from the first fruits of what you just reaped. How do you know when you are ready to reap? You know when supernatural faith enters in and you know that you know God has done it—not by hoping and pleading, but simply by receiving what has already been done. When you take the *leap of faith*, God comes through. Don't take a *leap of hope* or presume thinking it is faith. God has to place the faith in you supernaturally; it's not just something you confess.

Faith for receiving will start to grow by doing the act of sowing as you give God something to work with. *"Faith without works is dead"* (James 2:20b).

God said that even the angels would be used to reap the harvest in the last days. You can ask God to send angels to bring in the necessary funds and He will do it. Many times after we pray over an offering that was given to our ministry, people tell us later that thousands of dollars appeared in their bank account and the bank could not account for the reason. We have had people tell us that they received large, unexpected tax refunds, as well as had entire debts on homes, cars, ministries, churches, and credit cards paid off after we asked God to multiply what they had sown into His glory. We were told by a couple that money appeared on their doorstep, and others found envelopes of cash in their locked homes. Some businesspeople are reaping incredible increases that they in turn use as blessings for advancing the Kingdom of God.

Who provided the money? Angels are God's servants on the earth. An angel was used to stir the waters (see John 5:4). They can also be used to provide as well as to guide an unsaved person to a meeting or to someone who can lead him to the Lord. You can ask God to release provision and angels to do such things. I believe there is a head angel over finances. This angel represents the Lord who provides. These angels of provision are as real as the angels that protect us.

REAPING WHAT YOU DID NOT SOW

I have given you a land for which you did not labor, and cities which you did not build, and you dwell in them; you eat of the vineyards and olive groves which you did not plant (Joshua 24:13).

After you have been faithful to sow sacrificially and then purposely reap what you sowed, you can enter the next dimension: *reaping where you did not sow*. This is the realm of living in the over and above, where you go beyond your cup being filled to where your cup is running over. Few enter this realm, because they don't master the sacrificial sowing or the violent reaping dimension on a consistent basis. This is where things get exciting.

The Scriptures tell us about three men who were given talents. (See Matthew 25:14-30.) One received one talent, another two talents, and another five. As the story goes, two invested their talents: the man with five talents received an additional five; the man with two, another two. But the man who hid his one talent was rebuked and his talent was given to the man with the ten talents. Why? The man who doubled his five talents was faithful to sow and reap violently, so he entered the third dimension. He reaped where he did not sow! Once we grab hold of this revelation there will no longer be a shortage of finances for His Kingdom!

As you read previously in this chapter, when I gave away my car in obedience to a word from God, I later reaped a much nicer car. God also entrusted me with a much larger ministry through which I minister to thousands instead of to hundreds of people. Months after I received the new car, I was driving to Germany from France and meditating on this revelation of reaping where I have never sowed. I declared out loud that I would now reap where I have never sowed. I was thinking about reaping souls and nations I had never prayed for.

When I arrived in Germany, the same man who had given me the car invited me to his car dealership again. He told me to pick another car, but suggested which car he thought was the best one—a luxury version of the same car I had received the first time. I was baffled, and assumed he wanted to exchange it for the car he previously had given me. No, he told me to keep both cars! I was amazed and wondered why in the world this happened. I had not sowed a second car so how did I reap this one? I had not even been asking or praying for another car. The Lord showed me that because I had been faithful in violent sowing and reaping, I entered the next dimension of reaping where I had never sowed.

The key is to declare it with your mouth, "I reap where I have never sowed." After you declare it out loud, angels are released to hearken to the Word of God. When you declare the Word, angels can't distinguish between your voice and God's because it is *His Word.* They react as if He Himself is declaring it. That is the authority that comes when you declare a revelation from Heaven.

But now I had a problem. I could not drive two cars back to France. These are the new kinds of "problems" that arise when the "God of too much" begins to manifest as His glory increases. This is described in Moses' day when the people brought *"too much"* for the work of the temple (see Exod. 36:5-7). Later, God instructed me to give the second car to a fellow minister during a conference/crusade that we hosted. What a joy it was to be blessed in order to bless the socks off someone else!

Many of us serve the "God of just enough" instead of the "God of too much." We pray and ask God to provide just enough to pay the bills. We need to go beyond this way of thinking. The way you perceive God is often the way He will manifest. If you think He is the God of "just enough," you will aim your prayers and faith at that level. But, if you know that He provides above what you can ask or even imagine, then you will start to pray and believe differently. We serve a BIG God.

The purpose and motive for entering this realm must simply be to be a blessing to others. We must purge ourselves of any and all selfish desires to hoard or to follow certain principles of blessing out of a spirit of greed. The end result must be, "Lord, bless me so I can be a blessing to others and fulfill the call You have on my life."

REAPING THE WORLD'S WEALTH

The final and highest level of reaping in the material sense is reaping the wealth of the world or the sinner. This is the greatest wealth for the Kingdom of God. This level of blessing makes everything else pale in comparison. It's almost as if God has us practicing the first three levels in preparation for this one.

The Bible says that He will *give you the treasures of darkness and hidden riches of secret places..."* (Isa. 45:3). Those places are in the world. How can we receive or take in the wealth of the sinner? The Bible says that it is *laid up,* sitting there waiting for us. Other Scripture passages say that the sinner stores it up for us to inherit it for His Kingdom (see Prov. 13:22).

How do you reap from the world? The only way it works is if you sow into the earth that God created and the system that God put into place. Now when I say sow into the earth or world, I mean invest. God created the earth to produce and the world is profiting off of the system that God put into place. We too need to reap the earth's wealth instead of waiting for it to come from a fellow believer. Believers who do not invest in the present world can't reap from it.

For example, owning your own home is a big start. If you rent a home or apartment for 20 years, in most cases you are giving your wealth to an unsaved landlord rather than investing in your own property to leave for your children and family. The Bible mentions in the Book of Proverbs that *"a good man leaves an inheritance to his children's children"* (Prov. 13:22a). Make plans today to own your own home. With faith and consistent sowing, God will help you.

I believe that God wants the world's money to work for you instead of you working for the world's money. Basically, the key is buying and selling. Buy low and sell high. For instance, you can buy a used car at an auction and resell it for much more. Or you can buy a second home at a low price in an area where property values are increasing, such as a resort location. If you rent out the vacation home during the year at a higher rate than your mortgage payments, you will be increasing your income. There are tax advantages to owning investment property; and, depending on the housing market, you may also be able to sell the property for a profit.

Although I am not a professional investment counselor, I believe there are better ways to increase your talents than just letting your money sit in a savings account where it doesn't earn much interest. In addition to putting your money in savings, invest a portion in alternative areas. Ask a trusted and credible financial or banking consultant for advice. When you only save enough money for a rainy day, you are like the man with one talent who hid his money. Instead, be like the men with two and five talents who doubled their money by investing and without having to work for it.

Put your funds into something that will increase your money but does not require too much of your time. God may give you an invention, a skill, or a creative idea in which you can invest. The income from investing could eventually replace your "day job" and allow you to focus on the things God has called you to do instead of feeling forced to do a job that you know is not your ultimate calling. You may receive a prophetic direction to invest, for example, in a certain stock or real estate investment. Months later the stock may skyrocket and God may tell you to sell the shares or the real estate you bought—He will bless your obedience.

If you put your money in the right place at the right time, you will reap the wealth of the world and can then use it to expand His Kingdom. The widow who collected the jars of oil in the time of famine used the same principle. She bought low and sold high. She got the oil for free, and then the prophet gave her the word to go and sell the oil and pay off her debts. When we listen to the prophetic, we prosper. Unfortunately, many of God's people are in financial bondage and debt. He wants to give you a prophetic word and direction about how to get out of your famine and into His blessing. He is the same God today as the God who provided for Elijah more than 2,000 years ago. He continually cares about every area of our lives, including our finances.

RECIPE FOR REAPING

1. Give your tithes to God so He will protect you from the devourer.

2. Sow and reap abundantly into the glory.

3. Put at least 10 percent aside into a savings account or somewhere safe until you are ready to invest it.

4. Try to save at least three months' worth of living expenses as a job-loss buffer.

5. Invest and multiply the "leftover" money.

6. Sow again some of the money you reaped into ministries that are good ground. That way you are reaping from your giving into the Kingdom and reaping the wealth of the world at the same time. By doing this, you will have more and more to bless God with.

The Bible says that whatever your hand does will prosper (see Deut. 28:12), so find something profitable to do with your "hands." If your hands are not invested in a harvest, He can't bless it. He can't bless and multiply your investments, good works, talents, and/or crops if you aren't out there in the world using what He has already provided for you.

Also, prophetically declaring that the favor of the Lord is upon you and that the wealth of the sinner is stored up for the righteous will cause people in the world to favor you. When Israel left Egypt, they inherited all its wealth (see Exod. 12:35-36). They reaped what they should have earned all those years while in slavery, plus they reaped beyond what they had sowed. The Egyptians were compelled to bless them, though they were not God's people and were in fact outside of His covenant with Israel. I believe the world will also do this for us as the glory of God and the revelation continues to grow in the church.

The *Elijah anointing* is all about restoring to the church what was lost—restoring the power of God, gifts of God, promises of God, and the wealth of God.

Since the first Council of Nicaea in A.D. 325, when the church cut itself off from associating with the Jews, a poverty spirit emerged. It's interesting to note that the promise of blessing came to the Jewish people, and they walked in it even during this time when the church in Rome disassociated itself from God's chosen people.[1] I believe that when Christians separated themselves from their Jewish brethren they also cut themselves off from the Old Testament Scriptures promising His blessing in every area of their lives.

When the church cut itself off from the root of blessings and fellowship with Israel and the Jewish people who carried this revelation, it lost all of God's covenant promises to Israel concerning wealth. They instead believed their own doctrine that being poor is a sign of humility. Because the Jews were blessed with material wealth, Christians wrongly surmised that it was a sin to be blessed materially because of their hatred and jealousy of God's chosen people during that time. The root of this belief came from anti-Semitism.

As we believers come back to loving and supporting Israel and the Jewish people, who preserved the oracles and Word of God for the world, a double portion of blessing will also return as we tap into the rich and fertile promises of God. As we associate ourselves with God's covenant land and people, we also will receive the promises and covenants of blessing promised to the Jews, their children, and the Body of Christ, who are also children of Abraham by faith.

God is faithful, and His supernatural manifestations of provision will continue as we continue to be obedient—as was Elijah!

ENDNOTE

1. Henry R. Percival, ed., *The Seven Ecumenical Councils of the Undivided Church*, Vol. XIV of Nicene and Post Nicene Fathers, 2nd series, ed. Philip Schaff and Henry Wace, (Edinburgh: T&T Clark; Grand Rapids MI: Wm. B. Eerdmans, 1988).

CHAPTER SIX

GOVERNMENT GLORY

Nations will come to your light, and kings to the brightness of your rising (Isaiah 60:3 NASB).

As the spirit of Elijah increases, so will speaking His glory into governments increase—and they will be released in unprecedented ways. I know this is already happening, but soon it will occur at an accelerated pace. There will be so many prophets and apostles speaking to heads of nations that the government leaders will be unable to deny what God is saying to them. Prophetic signs and wonders will confirm what is being said.

The Church has often been satisfied with the prophetic gifts staying confined within their churches, home groups, or special conferences. But, these are only the starting places where there is room to learn and grow in these gifts. Unfortunately, many have allowed the prophetic gifts to stagnate on a lower level, blessing only each other with words. Now is the time for God to showcase His prophetic glory to the heads of nations. The Bible says in the Book of Proverbs, *"A man's gift makes room for him, and brings him before great men"* (Prov. 18:16). Now is the time for God to share this gift with the secular world so people will be confronted with God's Word and power. God greatly desires to speak to world leaders and those in positions of influence such as actors, athletes, bankers, and businessmen and women. People are desperately looking for answers to major worldwide crises. There needs to be enough vessels who are prepared, trained, trustworthy, and purified to carry out this task.

Moses spoke to the major world power of his day, Egypt. Not only did he go to the Pharaoh and prophesy, but he also moved in signs and wonders to support his words. I believe that this is the true Elijah glory of the last days. We need to prepare ourselves to do God's bidding on a grand, worldwide scale.

We cannot just give accurate prophetic words; they must be coupled with a signs and wonders ministry. Some messengers of God move more strongly in the prophetic, and others move more strongly in miracles, signs, and wonders. Both giftings are critical; where one is lacking, the other will be strong—a combination of the two is greater yet. These two groups need to connect and minister more together so as to benefit from the fullness of both.

Elijah prophesied that it would not rain for three and a half years, and then, that it would rain again. (See James 5:17-18; First Kings 18:41-45.) Elisha prophesied to Naaman, the commander of the Syrian army, that if he would dip seven times in the Jordan River he would be healed, and he was (see 2 Kings 5:1-14). Through Elijah and Elisha, God touched a world leader and a military commander of an enemy nation with prophetic words that brought miracles. Naaman had searched out Elisha. As the glory grows over modern-day prophets, world and community leaders will search out those of us who choose to obey God in this new expression of His glory.

The Bibles says in Isaiah 60:1 to *"Arise, shine; for your light has come! And the glory of the Lord is risen upon you."* As we arise and allow His glory to penetrate every part of our being, we will activate reactions in the world and the seats of governments. They will be drawn to search us out, as *His glory will appear upon us.* As this happens and His glory moves upon us, it will trigger a chain reaction. Isaiah 60:3 (NIV) says, *"Nations will come to your light, and kings to the brightness of your dawn."*

We must arise and keep rising so that the presidents, prime ministers, kings, governors, and mayors of the earth will search us out to hear from God and see His glory. David the shepherd boy knew this glory. He worshiped God in the fields with the sheep and practiced the presence of God. Sheep symbolically represent believers. God wants us to first practice the presence of God in our places of worship and our homes until it gets so strong that leaders search us out. As David grew in glory, he defeated the giant Goliath, although he was a small boy. Years later, word reached King Saul about a young man who could play the harp and drive evil spirits away. God promoted David above all his brothers who were naturally skilled, talented, and physically impressive. David was the one prophesied to be king—because he let the glory arise in him until it became evident.

BEING A VOICE

God has to do a major work in us in order for us to be able to handle such a task. We are often dealing not just with a particular leader, but also with the principalities and powers working behind that government position. We must be ready for such an assignment—going in unprepared spiritually could be suicide. Paul the apostle went to Cyprus and ministered to the key leader of the island, the proconsul. While doing so, he had major opposition from the sorcerer, Bar-Jesus, who tried to dissuade the proconsul just before his conversion. As mentioned previously, Paul prophesied that the sorcerer would become blind for three days (see Acts 13:6-12). That prophetic word, coupled with the sign of the sorcerer losing his sight, attested to the urgency and importance in God's heart of the leader's conversion. The enemy knew that if the leader became a believer, it would affect the entire nation of Cyprus, allowing freedom for the Gospel to be preached. This freedom would spread and touch other leaders in the Roman government and even affect laws regarding the Gospel. As Paul was ready to do God's bidding, we must be ready at all times.

We cannot have any ulterior motives for wanting to be used in this way. Selfish ambition, pride, insecurity, and greed can have no root in us. The people of authority we will be speaking to often deal with these issues. Our motive must simply be that God spoke and we are trying to obey what He has told us to do.

If we allow insecurity and false humility to control us, we may bail out at the last minute, feeling unworthy to speak to those in authority. We must remember, *"It is no longer I who live but Christ lives in me...*" (Gal. 2:20). Your identity has to be so changed that you don't look at your own stature, influence, or past identity. You must have a total transformation of identity that comes from being transformed by the presence and glory of Jesus. Peter had a total change of identity, having been with Jesus. He boldly confronted the religious leaders, urging them to repent, telling them that it was they who crucified the Lord. They were amazed at his boldness and authority, knowing he was unlearned and a simple fisherman from Galilee. His past identity did not stop Peter. Jesus gave him a new identity: *"fisher of men"!* (See Mark 1:17.)

I believe that one reason not many *"noble"* people are chosen to proclaim the Gospel (see 1 Cor. 1:26) is because they would be tempted to ride on their natural talents, persuasiveness, or influence. We need a new identity in order to walk into a new calling and level of glory. Lay down everything you think you are, or are not in the eyes of others, and let God resurrect you into a new creation. As you start to see yourself in His eyes and act that way, others will recognize a new authority in you and you will become a new person. Paul's identity changed as he encountered the glory on the road to Damascus. He was blinded for three days and became a changed man. His entire identity was transformed from a persecutor of the saints to one who became an apostle of the Lord. One powerful experience in His glory will change us, blind us to what we were, and open our eyes to a new calling and identity.

WHAT KINGS LOOK FOR

Kings can be government leaders as well as business executives, community and school officials, famous entertainers, religious leaders, or any person who has major influence over a nation, community, or people group.

Kings of the earth look for an Elijah who has a message or direction from God to answer their questions or solve their problems. You can be nice, polite, and politically correct, but if you don't have a Word from God and a solution, the king will soon realize that you are wasting his time. One word from God changes it all. Get in the spirit, flow in the glory of God, and listen for a Word from God. That is your main weapon that you can't leave home without. Although you can quote all the Scriptures, make sure God has spoken to you before approaching a king.

Earthly kings rule by giving directions, even though often they do not know what direction to take. Many people, nations, and communities depend on them to make the right decisions. Many times, kings search out those who can counsel and direct them in the right course through the supernatural. Many leaders are so desperate not to make a wrong decision that may result in nationwide consequences that they consult mediums, psychics, or sorcerers. These are the type of people you will be "competing with" when you approach an earthly king.

But one word from God is more powerful then 10,000 words from a sorcerer. King Saul consulted a sorcerer during his reign, which led to the end of his career and ministry. We owe it to our generation to proclaim the Word of the Lord. It is sad when a ruler of a nation cannot find or has not heard the Word of the Lord and is forced to rely on wicked ones to give him direction.

THE IMPORTANCE OF MOTIVES

Leaders also look for someone who is trustworthy, and without ulterior motives. When Naaman offered to give many material treasures to Elisha, he refused, because God told him not to take them. Maybe Naaman attempted to pay for the healing he received from Elisha's God because he had paid sorcerers in the past for their service; he may have thought that this relieved him of any debt that he owed God and the man of God. But Naaman's debt to the Lord God of Israel was worship only. Elisha's servant Gehazi, though, went back to Naaman, pretended that Elisha had changed his mind and wanted the material rewards, and took them and hid them in his own house, thus compromising his character and proving he was a double-minded man. (See Second Kings 5:20-27.)

Kings look for men and woman of God who are not ministering to them because of the potential material gain. If that is their motivation, they are no better than magicians or hirelings. For example,

I believe that the prophets of Jezebel had God-given prophetic gifts initially, but sold out to Jezebel for hire. When we prophesy, we need to have no other motive than simply to be the voice of God to that government official, media professional, entertainer, or school or business leader. Being the voice of God puts great authority upon you and nothing can deter you.

So first, we need a word from God; and second, we need to be trustworthy in order to be received by the kings of the earth. Being trustworthy is especially important when it concerns private or sensitive issues that would jeopardize the leader if your conversation were to become public.

If kings are led of the Lord to bless His servants in ways that increase His work, that is perfectly acceptable and appreciated—but it cannot be our motive. And we can't receive a gift if we feel it is being given as payment for our service or as a form of manipulation. We must discern between a gift given to God through us in thanksgiving to God, and a gift given with a control element involved in order to secure future words when needed, or given as payment for our help. Eventually, the kings will come and give their gifts and favor to advance the Kingdom of God, as Cyrus did.

> *...To you the riches of the nations will come...and their kings will serve you...so that men may bring you the wealth of the nations—their kings led in triumphal procession...You will drink the milk of nations and be nursed at royal breasts. Then you will know that I, the Lord, am your Savior, your Redeemer, the Mighty One of Jacob* (Isaiah 60:5,10-11,16 NIV).

God wants the wealth of kings to flow into the hands of His people, but in His way and His time. The Bible declares, *"The wealth of the sinner is stored up for the righteous"* (Prov. 13:22b).

STEPPING INTO GOVERNMENT GLORY

As mentioned in Chapter 4, as I was traveling from Paris to Gabon in Africa on my first visit to hold crusades and television interviews, the Lord told me to prepare to witness to the government in that country. This account is a continuation of my earlier reference to this visit and is explained in more detail about what went on behind the scenes.

When I arrived and the pastor asked me if there was anything that he could do for me, I asked him if he could secure a meeting with either the president or vice president of the country. He looked surprised, but the next week he called my hotel room and said, "Get dressed, in two hours you are meeting with the vice president of Gabon in his home."

Even though God had spoken this to me on the plane, I was amazed and asked the pastor how he arranged the meeting. He said he told the vice president that I was a prophet with a word from God and that he urgently needed to hear it. Because I never identified myself as a prophet, even though our ministry often moves very prophetically as God leads, I asked the pastor why on earth he told the vice president I had an urgent word for him. He said it was the only way he could set up a meeting where the vice president would listen.

The pastor asked, "Well, *do* you have an important prophecy or message directly from God?"

"No, not yet," I answered.

"Well, you better get one quick!" he said. I began to pray and ask God desperately for a word. I had the faith to believe for a meeting with the government official but totally forgot to pray about what I was supposed to say if this meeting really took place. God does not play around; if He says you will speak to so-and-so, you had better be prepared to take it seriously. I confessed, prayed, bound, praised, and almost begged. Finally the two hours were up and still no message from God.

What was I to say? Some poetic prophecy like "God loves you and has a wonderful plan for your life"? I wanted to be prophetic, not pathetic. This was a man who did not have time to waste. This was not the time to play a guessing game, such as asking him if his mother dropped him when he was six years old and then follow with, "God is healing your rejection." No, it's got to be better than that. The world often needs more proof that God is speaking.

I have learned the importance of upgrading prophetic gifts. Many of us are satisfied with the beginner's stage of the prophetic, such as describing a prophetic vision: "I see a vision. The sky is blue, you are in a boat, and the wind is blowing." Then when someone asks what it could mean, you simply respond by stating that you don't know, but that is what you saw. When God puts someone of high authority in your path and the destiny and direction of a nation, community, or organization could be at stake, it's time to believe God for more detailed words that a leader will quickly identify as being from God. I believe that within the church God provides a safe environment for believers to grow in the gifts, but when it's time to use them in the world, that is the time to demonstrate the power of God.

Finally, I had prayed all I knew to pray and wondered why I did not get a word. Suddenly, at the last moment the Lord spoke to me the word I was to give the vice president. I asked the Lord why He took so long to answer. He told me that He was waiting for me to stop talking so I could hear what He wanted to tell me. I could have gotten His word two hours earlier if I would simply have been still before Him and spent time listening, not continually requesting.

I told the vice president what God had told me: that he was second in command of the nation as were Joseph and Daniel, and that he would be tested in similar ways. Then I shared some personal things about his life and areas known only to him. I told him that if he would obey God in those areas, he would be further promoted. Also, there were warnings from God concerning certain things that only he and God could have known. When I finished sharing what God had told me, I prayed with him and his wife. The man began to weep in front of me and so did the wife.

They said that what I told them was a word directly from God and that they desperately needed to hear it exactly at that time. I was relieved and thanked God and them for their time. I left and asked God to confirm that I was not dreaming. Two hours later, Dr. David Yonggi Cho, the pastor of the largest church in the world, with over 700,000 members, met with the vice president. Dr. Cho was scheduled to conduct a crusade in Gabon's capital city where I had just ministered. He had flown in from South Korea, and after landing, headed straight for the home of the vice president. He sat exactly where I had sat two hours earlier, and he gave the vice president the exact same prophecy almost word for word. What a surprise the vice president must have had, and what amazing confirmation he had from God by God sending two different servants from totally different countries with the same message.

GATEWAYS IN THE SPIRIT

Similar incidents have happened in other countries. If God tells you to speak to government officials or other leaders, then declare it prophetically to yourself. As you do this, God will send angels, people, and circumstances to make the arrangements.

In another instance, as I was flying to Wanganui, New Zealand, to preach, the glory of God came upon me strongly to prophesy. The Lord told me to declare that the gates of the city were open for the King of glory to enter in. I did as I was commanded. When I arrived at the terminal, it was empty except for the pastor, who was waiting for me, and the mayor of the city. The Scriptures say that you meet the elders at the gates of the city. (See Joshua 20:4.) The gates during Bible days were points of entry into a city. Today, gates or points of entry include airports. At this airport (the physical gate), I met both the pastor (the spiritual gate) and the mayor (the political gate).

The pastor did not even know that the mayor was going to be there departing on a trip. I approached him and prophesied to him what the Lord had shown me for the city and his life. The mayor offered me his card and phone number and told me to call him if I needed anything and that he would make it happen.

In Bible days there were security checks to make sure no enemies entered cities. Today our identity and purpose of entry is also checked at modern-day ports of entry. This is where I met the spiritual and political "elders" of the city. Both are important gates that need to open to the purposes of God. The Lord had basically given me favor and the keys to the gates of the city. There was no hindrance in the spiritual or governmental realm.

We had a most wonderful week of meetings with many unusual creative miracles, such as a bald man receiving hair, numerous healings, angelic visitations, and many more miracles resulting in souls being saved each night. I know now that the words of the mayor welcoming me to the city were really welcoming the Holy Spirit and Jesus to do His purposes, and it made a big difference in the turnout and impact of the meetings.

More and more, my wife and I are invited to be interviewed on television—yet another gate or port of entry. When we are offered this opportunity, usually I will be led to prophesy over the airwaves the destiny of that city, nation, or individuals there. As you prophesy, the prophecy is formed and created as you speak. I've explained this in more detail in my book, *Mysteries of the Glory Unveiled.* During the meetings in the cities where we are interviewed, there is a phenomenal grace and blessing. When you speak over the airwaves, you are invading and taking back the space of the *"prince of the power of the air"* and displacing the enemy so that God can rule over the airwaves and bring His purposes to pass. This is another gate into the city. If you study the apostles, you will notice that they too went to the gates of the city to speak and to declare the oracles of God at the governmental and spiritual seats of power. They went to places where the entire city could listen to them, thereby spreading the message to the maximum number of people and also influencing the leadership of the cities.

If you are faithful to pray and even fast for the world, governments, and citywide leaders whom God puts on your heart, the Lord may very well open the door for you to speak into that situation. God may also use your prayers to open the way for you to give the word of the Lord to leaders in desperate need.

CHAPTER SEVEN

DELIVERANCE GLORY

One of the characteristics of the glory that the Elijah mantle carries is what I call *deliverance glory*. When the glory of God appears, deliverance happens quickly. In the glory, time does not exist as we consider it on the earth. "*One day is as a thousand years...*" (2 Pet. 3:8). The glory is an accelerator. What would normally take years happens in a moment in His glory. The Word of God says, "*Your will be done on earth as it is in heaven*" (Matt. 6:10). Well, how would things be in Heaven?

If you had a tumor and walked into Heaven, how long do you think it would take for you to be healed? On the same note, if you needed deliverance from something, how long would it take you to get it if you were in Heaven? Instantly, right? The reason: the glory that is in Heaven. In the glory there is no sickness or demons because in Heaven, they are not allowed to enter. If God's will is to be done *on the earth as it is in Heaven,* then the one ingredient missing from earth as it is in Heaven is the *glory*. When that glory appears on the earth, then we can say and expect with confidence that His will will be done as rapidly on the earth as it would be in Heaven.

In *Mysteries of the Glory Unveiled,* I mention how the glory comes. There are several ways to create an atmosphere for His glory to come. When it does come, deliverance happens in a much faster way than without His glory appearing.

King David learned this lesson when he played the harp for Saul. He knew how to tap into the glory realm through praise and worship, which is very powerful. In fact, David was known to play the harp with skill, and the special presence of God that resided on his skill manifested when he played. Saul was tormented with evil spirits and needed relief. He called on David to play the harp, and while he did, Saul would be relieved of the tormenting spirits. The reason: true worship leads to the glory and presence of God, which appears in response to worship. When the Lord Himself appears in His glory or brings His presence, evil flees.

Arise, shine; for your light has come! And the glory of the Lord is risen upon you. For behold, the darkness shall cover the earth, and deep darkness the people; but the Lord will arise over you, and His glory [light] will be seen upon you (Isaiah 60:1-2).

LET THERE BE LIGHT

Light expels darkness by its very nature. When the lights are on, there is no darkness. If you try to cast away darkness, but you yourself are not full of light, chances are it will take you a long time to do it.

When you are full of the glory of God, often one word alone from God will expel the darkness. Jesus came to the man with the legion of devils. The man had broken off all his chains, and the whole region feared him. With just one word from Jesus, the man was totally freed. (See Mark 5:1-20.) The less you are filled with the glory of God, the longer it takes to cast out darkness or to see deliverance and victory in spiritual warfare. The real warfare takes place when you remain in the glory; once there, the Lord fights on your behalf.

The disciples struggled over casting out the spirit from the boy who kept throwing himself in the fire. They failed to free him. Jesus had been praying and fasting all night on the mountain. He came and cast out the spirit from the boy and then corrected the disciples, explaining the need for faith and prayer and fasting. (See Matthew 17:14-21.)

Fasting is another way to get into the glory more quickly. The more of His glory that is in you, the less effort it takes to expel darkness. Less glory will lead to more of you trying to do the job in your own strength. That is why deliverance and warfare are usually very tiring. We need more of *His glory,* and then, less intervention on our part will be required.

When I was in Africa preaching in a crusade, there were many people desperately in need of deliverance. I ministered on the glory of God, and during the open-air outdoor meeting, a demon-possessed woman approached the stage hissing like a cat. My knee-jerk reaction was to cast it out so as not to allow it to disrupt the meeting. But then again, I did not want the focus of the meeting to shift to the devil and to this woman when the people were so close to the glory and were worshiping the Lord with all their hearts.

The Lord told me I had two options. I could bind the spirit and she would calm down, but the crowd's focus would be on her. My other option was to keep the people worshiping; then, as the glory increased, the Lord Himself would deliver not only her but also the entire crowd. I chose the latter. The woman got closer and closer to the stage, but I just ignored her and kept the people singing.

Suddenly I was singing a new song. The song went something like this: "In Heaven's glory there are no demons or darkness, Your will be done on earth as it is in Heaven." As I began to sing, I could see angels descending upon the people from a portal in Heaven. As I pointed in the direction where the angels were, hundreds of people on that side of the crusade suddenly fell to the floor, screaming, vomiting, and coughing as deliverances took place while I was singing. Then I pointed to another direction where I saw angels, and hundreds more on that side of the stage fell with the same deliverance manifestations. Those involved in witchcraft, freemasonry, generational curses, and the like were being gloriously set free. This went on for about two hours. I never had to huff and puff and scream, or go through all the deliverance techniques some use during one-on-one deliverances. Mass deliverances were taking place while we were worshiping and singing.

When I sang, "There are no demons in the glory in Heaven," the demons had to leave. Demons know they cannot enter Heaven and realized that with the glory coming down, the same rules applied. Imagine hundreds of people instantly delivered as the glory invaded. I didn't have to ask the demon's name and all his relatives' names before they went. All that was needed was to bring the glory down and let God do it His way.

The only problem was that the demon-possessed lady approaching me on the stage did not budge. I simply asked that the angels working the crowds would come to the stage to accompany and minister to this woman. As soon as I spoke, the woman began pointing to the angels on her right and then on her left as she screamed in fear. She fell on her back and her legs began kicking violently as if someone was pinning her down. The kicking stopped and she was set free, normal, and in her right mind.

As the music played and people worshiped, we heard in the background hundreds of people screaming as mass deliverances were taking place. At the end of this, many souls ran up to the front to be saved. Even people a mile away heard the screams and came to watch—they too ran up to be saved. That night there was almost no preaching except during the salvation call at the end; yet many gave their hearts to the Lord after seeing the deliverances and the glory of God. This is *deliverance glory*. The glory is an accelerator and speeds up the process.

God uses angels in the process of deliverance. The more of the glory there is, the more angelic beings are present. When a king or leader comes into a room, there are bodyguards and an entourage. The same happens when the glory appears; God has an entourage of heavenly hosts. These hosts will secure an area much like when a country's president appears in a public place. They will ensure that darkness and danger are removed to prepare for the president's arrival. Angels, having just left Heaven to accompany the glory, radiate with heavenly-presence light, and much darkness is expelled when they are present.

When Elisha faced the entire Syrian army, which was looking for him to capture and kill him, he had a similar experience (see 2 Kings 6:8-17). His servant was frightened, seeing that they were outnumbered. Elisha prayed, asking God to open the eyes of his servant. When He did, the servant could see multitudes of armies of angels aligned in the heavens ready to fight on their behalf. Then he knew they were not outnumbered but were actually in the majority. In Acts

1:8, God promised to release the power of His Holy Spirit on us. He has thousands of angels at His disposal, so we do too! (See Matthew 26:53.) If we could only perceive the army of angels that God has placed at our disposal to dispel darkness and enemy forces, we would never fear anything again. The secret is to stay in His presence, in the secret place, so that His glory becomes our guard. *"He who dwells in the secret place of the Most High shall abide under the shadow of the Almighty"* (Ps. 91:1).

I was in French Guiana a few years ago when this realization became a reality to me. At a certain point in the service, there were hundreds of people requesting prayer. It was hot, as Guiana is located on the equator, and with no air conditioning, we were sweating profusely. I asked the Lord how in the world were we to pray for all the people, and He told me to use my ministry team. The problem: I did not bring my own team with me on this trip. The Holy Spirit then opened my eyes and showed me that I had a large *angelic* ministry team. He instructed me to walk among the people but not to touch them so that His ministering spirits could do the job.

As I obeyed and walked among the people, the power of God touched them, knocking many to the floor as they received miracles and deliverance; others went into trances during which they had visions of Heaven for several hours. Some said that they had been to Heaven and they recounted the things that God spoke to them. God did this work through angels.

When He was betrayed in the Garden of Gethsemane, Jesus said He could have called legions of angels to deliver Him from the suffering He was to endure. But He chose not to and obeyed God. (See Matthew 26:53-54.) Just before Jesus prayed in such agony that His sweat became like drops of blood falling to the ground (see Luke 22:44), an angel appeared and ministered to Him (see verse 43). He surely needed the strength for the day that lay ahead of Him. Jesus said that all power has now been given to us (see Matt. 10:1). I believe we also have access to legions of angels if the need ever arises—a legion is technically 3,000 to 6,000. We need to make room and allow these heavenly hosts to do much of the work on His behalf for us.

More and more we need to learn to operate in the glory realm His way and to let His hand touch the people. Often we get in the way, wanting to do all the work, when He can do it so much better and faster—with longer lasting results. Ask God to use you in deliverance glory, to see not just people but entire cities and nations freed from darkness into His glory.

ABUNDANCE AND GLORY

CHAPTER EIGHT
WAIT UNTIL THE SPIRIT MOVES

We understand that when the glory comes we have to act, obey, and let God do what He intends to in that glory. Now you may be asking, "How do I get the glory to come?"

There are several things that open up the glory realm. *Holiness* is one of them. In fact, in Pensacola, Florida, through an emphasis on holiness, the realm of glory was opened to such an extent that revival continued for years; it caused thousands to be saved and brought millions into one level of glory. The same could be said for Charles Finney and many of the past revivals, as people pursued this holiness portal into one dimension of His presence. Pursue holiness so you can stay in His glory and keep the channels and intimacy with God open.

Praise and worship quickly transports you into an atmosphere of the glory of God. It's not just any old way of praising that will open up the glory realm to us. There is a pattern in Heaven, and when the pattern is followed here on earth, it releases the glory. If the pattern is wrong, you don't get the same glory. The Bible talks about praise and then worship. Basically, you should praise until the spirit of worship comes. What is praise? I am talking about the fast-tempo songs that make you dance, jump, and shout to the Lord—breakthrough praise. Even adding a shofar blast in a meeting can add to the breakthrough. Keep praising until the spirit of worship comes.

When the spirit of worship comes, you will notice that you and those in the crowd don't feel like shouting or dancing any more. You feel more like loving on God, singing intimate slow songs of love to

Him. As you continue, you will sense the thick, heavy presence of God. That is the glory. Once the glory comes, just stand and soak in that glory. Don't stop short of the greater glory of God and settle for something lightweight. Most services, including those in revival and renewal, often mix up the worship with a worship song here and a praise song there, without following the pattern. The pattern is important—it is the pattern of Heaven. Skillful playing and singing are secondary. What use is it to have the most skilled singers and musicians if they don't usher in the glory of God. Only in His glory does the miraculous happen, which we pray for. Follow the pattern even in your home and the same glory will come. I recommend reading Ruth Heflin's first book, *Glory,* for more information on this subject of praise and worship that ushers in His glory.

The third way to usher in the glory is *fasting and prayer.* When you fast and pray you can break through into the glory realm at an accelerated pace. Why? The glory of God was very strong in the Garden of Eden, but the desire for forbidden food caused that glory to be cut off from man for the first time. When you fast, you usher back in that glory as you deny food for more of God. You are, in a sense, telling God that His glory is more important to you at that time than even food. That is why Jesus said, *"I have food to eat of which you do not know"* (John 4:32).

Fasting propels your spirit into the glory much like the rocket boosters and the enormous power that propel a space shuttle into orbit. Once in that realm you tend to hear God better, the power and presence of God increases upon you, and your faith deepens if you are spending that time in prayer, praise, and the Word. Your spirit is totally focused on the spirit realm, and distractions tend to lose their grip. That is why Jesus, the apostles, Moses, Elijah, and most of the patriarchs had a life of fasting and prayer with such phenomenal results that they shook nations and saw impossibilities become realities. I highly recommend Mahesh Chavda's book, *The Hidden Power of Prayer and Fasting,* to go deeper into this subject.

Another key to ushering in the glory is *sacrificial giving.* It opens up the glory and miracles in ways that nothing else will. There are countless testimonies confirming this throughout the Scriptures, from Genesis through Revelation. The Book of Malachi says that the *"windows of heaven"* open when there is a spirit of sacrificial giving.

> *"Bring all the tithes into the storehouse, that there may be food in My house, and try Me now in this," says the Lord of hosts, "if I will not open for you the windows of heaven and pour out for you such blessing that there will not be room enough to receive it"* (Malachi 3:10).

The widow who gave her last meal to Elijah multiplied her blessings, and her son was raised from the dead. Many of these examples are in my book, *Mysteries of the Glory Unveiled.* When these open doors of glory are together at the same time, it causes an explosion of glory. When these elements are mixed together in a ministry or at a meeting, there will be a major glory explosion leading to visitations from Heaven's throne, signs and wonders, revival, harvest, and an eternity full of His blessings.

WHEN THE SPIRIT MOVES

Now that we know some of the ways to prepare an atmosphere for the glory to come, how do we get the glory of God to manifest? Have you ever been in a meeting where the glory and power of God were so strong that you felt sure that miracles would take place, but still nothing happened? You left with the presence of God all over you but you could not figure out why the glory of God did not manifest. Because the glory of God is present, many make the mistake of immediately praying for the sick, casting out spirits, and inviting people to the altar. Many times the results are less spectacular compared to what could have been had they waited for the *moving* of the Spirit, not just the *coming* of the Spirit. It is one thing to get the glory and Spirit of God to come; it is another thing to get Him to move.

Some church leaders are so focused on getting God to come down that they have no revelation about His moving. On the other hand, some try to get God to move, but if He has not fully come or He is not yet giving the direction to move, I guarantee you He will not move. Once the glory comes, there are ways God chooses to operate in order for Him to move. The Bible says, *"The earth will be filled with the knowledge of the glory of the Lord, as the waters cover the sea"* (Hab. 2:14).

The earth will not be filled with just the glory but with the *knowledge of the glory.* If you don't have the knowledge of something, you will have trouble seeing it operate. In Second Samuel 6:6-7, the priests who should have been carrying the ark found this out the hard way. When the oxen pulling the wagon that was carrying the ark stumbled, and the ark started to fall, one of the Levites tried to fix the problem himself and was struck dead! Somehow the Israelites were able to have the ark of the glory in their midst but they did not have revelation about the ways of God and how He moves and operates.

The Book of Genesis describes the moving of the Spirit:

> *In the beginning God created the heavens and the earth. The earth was without form, and void; and darkness was on the face of the deep. And the Spirit of God was hovering over the face of the waters* (Genesis 1:1-2).

In the beginning we see the Spirit of God *"hovering"* or moving. We must not just get the glory or Spirit to come; we have to wait until He moves! He does not wait until we move; we have to wait until He is moving before we move. When He moves, we can move, and great miracles will occur. How do you know He is moving? It is similar to the wind—you know when the wind is moving even though you can't see it. You can *sense* when the wind is moving.

Our sensitivity to His moving needs to be developed. As soon as the Spirit began to move over the waters, as told in the Book of Genesis, then God spoke, *"Let there be light'; and there was light"* (Gen. 1:3). We have to wait until the Spirit moves before we declare things, pray for miracles, or take great steps of faith. Once the Spirit has moved, then you step out in faith and do or say that which God is doing or saying while He is moving. After the presence of God's glory has moved, you can be sure that God has already gone before you to perform what you will say or do. Now you can pick the fruit.

In our meetings we always try to wait until the Spirit is really moving before we pray for any miracles. Then great miracles occur. I remember when I was in New Zealand. The Spirit started to move and God told me to call out that baldness was healed. At the end of the meeting, a 72-year-old man who had been totally bald had hair appear on his head; he still has a full head of hair as of the time of this writing. These kinds of things happen when the Spirit is moving. We have seen this same miracle of instant hair growth occur several times in the United States and Europe.

We see this same "wait until the Spirit moves" principle in the pool of Bethesda healing. The paralytic explains to Jesus that an angel comes every now and then and stirs the waters. When the waters are stirred, whoever gets in the pool first is healed. (See John 5:1-8.) The stirring of the waters seems like the Spirit hovering over the waters in Genesis. When you wait until the Spirit moves before acting in faith, you will have victory. Using your faith is not the only thing needed— we need to use our faith at the right timing.

In First Kings 18:41, Elijah prophesied that it was going to rain. He sent his servant out several times to see if clouds or rain had arrived on the horizon. Finally, when the servant checked the seventh time, a cloud the size of a man's hand had formed! When Elijah sensed that the Spirit had started to move to bring the prophecy to pass, he began to act. He told Ahab to get in his chariot quickly and go fast before the rainstorm hit! (See First Kings 18:43-45.) Imagine that there has been a famine and no rain for years, and someone tells you to get off of the mountain because of the coming rainstorm— and all you see is a tiny little cloud. But Elijah knew that when the Spirit starts to move, you better move as well or you could miss your day of visitation.

I was in my room one day praising, worshiping, and praying until the Shekinah glory of God filled my room. I kept pressing in until I felt the Spirit of God moving. The Holy Spirit told me to emphatically declare that London, England, would open up for the glory of God. I did exactly that. Suddenly the telephone rang during my prayer time. It was an invitation to minister in London at Kensington

Temple. As the Spirit moved, the door was already opened; I only had to declare what God had already prepared when the Spirit moved.

Another time, I was in London preaching in a large African church. During the meeting I told the people that the Spirit was moving and that anyone who was sick or needed a miracle should get up and run. Hundreds of people got up and started running around the room. In that meeting, tumors dissolved, gold teeth fillings appeared, and many other miracles took place. There was a man in the back who was in a wheelchair, paralyzed from the waist down. He also had kidney failure and cancer, and had been told that he had only a short time left to live. The man could see that the Spirit was moving, although it was his first time in church. He was not even a believer. But, he told himself he had nothing to lose and he stood up and began to run with the other people while the Spirit was moving. He was totally healed that night. He gave his life to the Lord and was still healed years later when I followed up with him.

When David went to fight the Philistines and inquired of the Lord whether or not he should fight and how to do it, the Lord appeared to him and told him to wait until he could hear the sound of marching in the tops of the mulberry trees. Again, this waiting for the Spirit to move was a sign to David when to fight. David won the battle that day as he waited until the Spirit moved before acting. (See Second Samuel 5:23-25.) When the Spirit moves, you move with it. Don't wait until tomorrow. If the Spirit moves on you now to do something or call someone, pray for someone, or give to someone, do it as the Spirit is moving if you want miraculous results.

HOW TO INVITE THE SPIRIT TO MOVE

Now you know how to get the glory to come and how to wait until He moves. But you might be wondering if there is anything you can do to facilitate the moving of the Spirit. Is there anything you can do while you are waiting for Him to move to speed things up? Yes there is! Keep doing whatever you did to get Him to come in the first place and soon you will sense when He is moving. While you are waiting, keep praising, fasting, praying, giving, etc., until He moves. This is a discipline that in time will train your spiritual senses so that you can discern the slightest moving of His Spirit.

Paul and Silas were in prison and needed the Spirit to move on their behalf. They did not just sit there while waiting for God to move; they continued praising Him until the glory and Spirit of God came and moved. When the Spirit moved, they knew it, because the earth also moved and shook, and the prison doors were opened! (See Acts 16:16-26.)

In the environment of praying, praising, fasting, and seeking God as they had done since Pentecost in Acts 2, they had a new manifestation of the glory in Acts 4:29-31: not only did the Spirit come but it also moved, and the earth moved and the building shook! It is well worth waiting for the Spirit to move, and while waiting, to keep the doors of glory open by fasting, praying, praising, repenting, and giving.

Amazingly enough, it is recorded in Acts 4:32-35 that the believers started giving sacrificial gifts to the apostles, including the proceeds of the property and land that they had sold. This stirred the Holy Spirit to keep moving in the early church until there was not one who lacked among them. Then, in the next chapter of Acts, Peter's shadow alone healed the sick—going beyond the laying on of hands (see Acts 5:15-16). The early believers went from glory to glory once they knew how to wait until the Spirit moved!

The prophets often had someone play the harp or another instrument to get the Spirit moving before they would prophesy. (See Second Kings 3:14-16.) Then, when they did prophesy, it shook Heaven and earth, as entire nations were changed. I'm not suggesting that the gifts of the Spirit can only operate at specific times. Rather, I believe that if you wait on your gifts until the glory comes, when you do share them, the effects will be powerfully life-changing and situation-changing. Instead of just using your gift under your anointing, when you wait until He gives you the signal, then Heaven's glory will back it up and make it a hundred times more powerful.

Many people minister out of their gift instead of out of God's glory. The glory and presence of God comes first, then the gift. Be sure not to get the order mixed up if you want to see what the apostles saw and experience the next move of God's glory upon the earth.

CHAPTER NINE

RESURRECTION GLORY

As it was in the days of Elijah, Elisha, and Jesus, so today we are going to see a new release of resurrections as never before. Jesus commanded His disciples to raise the dead, heal the sick, and cleanse the lepers—all in the same command. He didn't say to only heal the sick, but when it comes to raising the dead, you really better think twice. No. Raising the dead is mentioned in the same way as healing the sick and casting out demons. Today's church has relegated resurrection ministry to the "not relevant" category, believing that it only happened in the days of the early church or might happen once in a lifetime, or occasionally in far-off, poor, developing countries.

In Ephesians, Paul prays that:

> ...the God of our Lord Jesus Christ, the Father of glory, may give to you the spirit of wisdom and revelation in the knowledge of Him...and what is the exceeding greatness of His power toward us who believe, according to the working of His mighty power (Ephesians 1:17,19).

The Lord will not only release His power to us, but He also will release revelation in order for us to know the *workings* of His power. It's no use having power without the knowledge of how to use it. I believe that God is revealing revelation knowledge in these days so believers will know not just the power but how the power works—even for raising the dead.

God is restoring everything in these days and will do so with even greater power. The spirit of Elijah will once again be fully resurrected in our day! *"Behold, I will send you Elijah the prophet before the coming of the great and dreadful day of the Lord"* (Mal. 4:5).

We know that the first major resurrections recorded involved Elijah and Elisha, and that the pattern continued with Jesus, and eventually, the Church. It is interesting to study the resurrections recorded in the Bible. In two similar circumstances, both Elijah and Elisha raised the dead in similar fashion. It would behoove us to learn from those who have already raised the dead.

> *And he stretched himself out on the child three times, and cried out to the Lord and said, "O Lord my God, I pray, let this child's soul come back to him." Then the Lord heard the voice of Elijah; and the soul of the child came back to him, and he revived* (1 Kings 17:21-22).

This major miracle in Elijah's ministry launched him into a new realm. When Elisha was confronted with the same situation later in his ministry, he had had a great mentor and naturally raised the dead in the same way he had seen his spiritual father do it. Elijah was the only one he could have learned from—as is often the case today, since we learn from those who disciple us.

Look carefully at the next passage and see how Elisha raised the dead. This passage gives us more details than the previous account.

> *And he went up and lay on the child, and put his mouth on his mouth, his eyes on his eyes, and his hands on his hands; and he stretched himself out on the child, and the flesh of the child became warm. He returned and walked back and forth in the house, and again went up and stretched himself out on him; then the child sneezed seven times, and the child opened his eyes* (2 Kings 4:34-35).

There are several keys to raising the dead, as written about in Elijah and Elisha's experiences. Both of them stretched out their bodies on the dead boys. The Scripture explains that Elisha put his mouth on the boy's mouth, as well as his eyes and hands on the boy's eyes and hands. Why in the world would someone put his mouth on a dead person's mouth? Today this procedure is known as mouth-to-mouth resuscitation, which sometimes works to revive a person who has stopped breathing. But where did this idea originate?

Life was breathed into man's nostrils by God. (See Genesis 2:7.) God symbolically put His face to Adam's face and brought life to him. This Genesis account may have been a source of direction, revelation, and inspiration for Elijah.

What God did was breathe "spirit" into man. A person with only a body but no human spirit has no life. Life is in the spirit of a person. When someone dies, the spirit of the person departs from the body. If the human spirit returns to the body, life returns. We see this principle in Ezekiel.

> *Also He said to me, "Prophesy to the breath, prophesy, son of man, and say to the breath, 'Thus says the Lord God: Come from the four winds, O breath, and breathe on these slain, that they may live.'"' So I prophesied as He commanded me, and breath came into them, and they lived, and stood on their feet, an exceedingly great army* (Ezekiel 37:9-10).

The word *breath* in God's command to the prophet also means "spirit" when translated from the original Hebrew. The spirit of a man or woman returning to his or her body is the key to raising the dead. That is why Elijah prayed, *"O Lord...let this child's soul come back to him."* He was calling the child's spirit back into his body. Often, today's translations of the Bible are not as accurate as they could be, and we lose much of the revelation we could be using.

The differences between translations became clear to me when I was preaching in Quebec, Canada. Before, as I was reading Ezekiel 37 from an English Bible, it said He commanded *breath;* but in the French Bible it says He commanded their *spirit* to return to them, not just their breath. As I was preaching, I received a revelation. I preached this revelation as it was coming to me while on the pulpit. All of a sudden, a glory for raising the dead was released into the room—I could sense it so strongly. During the service, a boy crippled from birth walked for the first time in his life. Later in the meeting,

I prophesied over an evangelist in the church and told him, "Greater things will you do; soon you will raise the dead."

Five days later, the man I prophesied to was in the hospital to have a growth removed. While in the operating room waiting for the surgery to begin, a dead woman was brought into his room. They tried to revive her, but nothing worked. Then it struck him. The man remembered my prophecy about him soon raising the dead. He had also received revelation about how to do it, as I had preached about that with a new revelation. In front of the five French Canadian doctors he yelled out to the dead woman to come back and commanded that her life (or spirit) return to her in the name of Jesus. He declared this twice. I can only imagine what the doctors were thinking—they might have thought he was in the wrong kind of hospital. Then suddenly the lady opened her eyes, took a deep breath, and was alive. The doctors were shocked and thanked the man for his help.

One revelation from God is all it takes to see a new manifestation of His abundant glory. Don't ever forget that a new revelation brings a new manifestation of God. We need to continually seek God for fresher and clearer revelation into the things of God for a greater and more powerful manifestation of God's glory in the world in these last days.

Another time, I was holding an outdoor crusade in Africa. During the service I received a word from the Lord that a lady in the crowd had come to the meeting by faith, yet her daughter was dying in a nearby hospital. Then I received a word from the Lord that the girl had just died but that we were to pray her back to life from where we were. When I spoke that word out, the mother began to weep. From the pulpit I commanded the spirit of the girl to come back into her body even though she was not physically at the meeting.

After the service the mother ran to the hospital to see what had become of her daughter. The doctor said that while the mother was gone, she had died and was no longer breathing; he then explained that they realized later she had come back to life. Time wise, she started breathing shortly after we began commanding her spirit to come back into her body. In this case, I did not personally need to be in the same room to see the dead raised. Since there is no distance in the Spirit, or the glory, we can command things to happen that are far away from us. Jesus commanded the Roman centurion's servant to be healed without setting foot in his house—and that same hour his servant was healed (see Matt. 8:5-13).

NOT DEAD, ONLY SLEEPING

Our friend Lazarus sleeps, but I go that I may wake him up (John 11:11b).

How could Jesus tell the people that Lazarus was not dead, when clearly, by all human measures, he was as dead as any other corpse? What was the revelation behind all this and how did He raise him from the dead? Earlier in the passage Jesus said that the sickness was not unto death but was for the glory of God. Lazarus was Jesus' friend. He, along with Lazarus' sisters Mary and Martha, spent much time together. Lazarus was well acquainted with the power and life of Jesus.

One day while I was preaching in one of our miracle campaigns, this revelation hit me right before I went up to the microphone— Jesus was able to speak to Lazarus even though he was physically dead. How was Jesus able to speak to him? Because Lazarus knew Jesus! After the life of Jesus touches a life and breathes on it, it can never die. Because you have a living, personal relationship with the Messiah, you will never die. Lazarus was not dead—he knew Jesus. All Jesus needed to do was wake him up from his sleep. The proof that he was not dead, at least in the spiritual sense, is that Lazarus responded by obeying Jesus and came back into his body.

Anything that God has breathed upon that seems dead is actually not dead but only sleeping or in a spiritual coma! Because Lazarus' life was totally devoted to God's Kingdom, Jesus could easily pull him from Heaven to earth. When God has touched something in your life, it never dies, even if it seems like it is not moving. Has God spoken or prophesied some things over your life that once had life and now seem dead? Did God use you powerfully in a certain way, and now it seems to be lost or gone? Those gifts and prophecies are not dead. If

God ever breathed upon an area of your life, it is not dead, only sleeping. Wake it up! Did God heal you and you seem to have lost that healing? It is not lost, only sleeping, because He has already touched it. Maybe you have unfulfilled promises. If they were "God-breathed," then they are not dead.

Abraham had faith that God would raise Isaac from the dead even if he had to go through with killing him as a sacrifice. (See Genesis 22:1-18.) Why? Because he knew that God had already breathed life and destiny on the boy, that God cannot lie, and that God is life even in the face of death.

Even the promise to give Abraham a son at his extraordinarily advanced age had to come to life. His body and the body of his wife were *"as good as dead"* (see Heb. 11:11-12); yet God spoke life to their bodies, and a son, Isaac, was born. There is nothing that God has ever touched that appears dead that God can't awaken. Believers in the Kingdom of God never really die, as we are now made alive in Christ, whether in the body or Spirit.

I believe as you read this that God is revealing some things and promises to you that you thought God had forgotten about or allowed to die. He is just waiting for you to realize the revelation that your dream, prophecy, revelation, desire, or miracle is not dead—only sleeping! He is ready to awaken those promises as you open yourself to His abundant glory.

Even cities and countries that once had major revivals and now seem dead are not dead, because the ashes of that revival still remain in the ground. In France, for example, thousands died as martyrs for their faith during the Protestant Reformation. They were called the French Huguenots. France, a country many have identified as spiritually dead, has never been dead—only sleeping. It is now awakening, with major miracles being witnessed, souls being saved, and churches growing—there is life from the dead despite the problems there.

There is a suburb of Paris called St. Denis where the World Cup Soccer tournament was played. In the subway station there is a statue of a man holding his head in his hand; his name is Saint Denis. He was a believer who preached with such conviction that the religious leaders of his day had him beheaded. It is written that Saint Denis picked up his head and walked several miles from the place of execution back to the very church that ordered his death. I believe he was not really dead, because he had been touched by God! God has manifested His *resurrection glory* in times past in different ways. Today is no different, because God never changes.

THE SAME YESTERDAY, TODAY, AND TOMORROW

Across the United States, Europe, and many other Western nations, the abundant glory and power of God is once again resurrecting and waking up what was and continues to be.

Several years ago I ministered in Spokane, Washington, where John G. Lake once ministered healing to the whole city. People came to his healing rooms, where they would be prayed for and remained until they were healed. Everyone who entered left healed. At that time Spokane was rated the healthiest city in America by secular standards. I visited John G. Lake's gravesite; there is a pine tree growing right through his grave. While preaching, I saw a vision of John G. Lake being raised from the dead. The Lord showed me that his anointing and ministry did not die when he passed away and that it would be resurrected if someone would just pick up the mantle that is lying on the ground in Spokane.

The glory that touched the city and seemed to have faded away is actually sleeping, waiting for someone else to wake it up. A short time later I learned that someone had bought the original property and renamed it the "healing rooms," and that the healing ministry of John G. Lake is continuing today right where it started! In fact, now there are churches all over the country that have healing rooms. The mantle never died; it just waited for someone with the revelation to awaken it. After God has breathed on an area, a city, a ministry, or anything, it only sleeps, never dies. Wake it up! Stir up the gifts that are in you and stir up the mantles over your region.

God is unleashing the *Elijah glory* with resurrection power to raise bodies, ministries, families, and nations from the dead!

RESURRECTION GLORY AND ISRAEL

The early church walked at a level of resurrection glory and power that we have yet to see. What was their secret? How did they tap into this *extreme glory?*

The Bible talks about the spirit of Elijah being restored in the last days.

> *Behold, I will send you Elijah the prophet before the coming of the great and dreadful day of the Lord. And he will turn the hearts of the fathers to the children, and the hearts of the children to their fathers, lest I come and strike the earth with a curse* (Malachi 4:5-6).

Here we see that the return of the spirit of Elijah is connected to the hearts of the fathers turning to their children and the children to their fathers. The Jewish people are the spiritual fathers of the faith. The Gentile Church today is made up of the children and offspring of the Jewish apostles and prophets. We have been disconnected from each other for over 2,000 years. As we are reconnected to each other, it will unlock the resurrection power of God that the early church walked in.

As mentioned previously, the Church was cut off from its Jewish roots in A.D. 325 during the Council of Nicaea, and ever since that time, the power and visitation of God have turned way down compared to how they were manifested in the early church. I believe they were actually lifted from the Church for a long season. As we reconnect to the Jewish roots of the Gospel, we will draw once again from the rich soil of God's power. Paul clearly demonstrates this in his writings in the Book of Romans.

> *For if their being cast away is the reconciling of the world, what will their acceptance be but life from the dead?* (Romans 11:15)

Here we see Paul talking about raising the dead in connection with Israel and the Jewish people being restored to salvation in their God.

Basically, when Israel, the root, is restored to the Messiah, and we are connected to that root of Israel and our Jewish forefathers, it will be *as the raising of the dead* for us and for our ministries. God is about to unleash a wave of resurrection glory to ministries and churches that will reconnect to the root and help Israel return to her Messiah. They will be accepted as they come as well as have a hedge of protection. The early church started with all Jewish believers and later opened to Gentiles. That dynamic allowed for an explosion of God's power as the two became one in Him.

A flower cut from its roots can only survive two days before it starts to die. The Church today has been uprooted and on its own for 2,000 years without its connection to Israel. We think we can continue the way we have been; but the third day is coming, and we cannot survive unless we get reconnected to our Jewish roots, from where the Church originated. (See Romans 11:16-18.) A day is as a thousand years to the Lord—we are now entering the third day.

On the third day Jesus rose from the dead. Ministries that are not reconnecting to Israel and its revival and influencing their followers to pray for Israel, bless her, and prepare her for the coming harvest, will start to die out; and their anointing, blessing, and favor will dry up with it. Those who are beginning to root themselves back into Israel, and are praying and supporting the revival of Israel, will be part of a third-day wave of great resurrection glory, power, favor, prosperity, and harvest!

> *I say then, have they stumbled that they should fall? Certainly not! But through their fall, to provoke them to jealousy, salvation has come to the Gentiles. Now if their fall is riches for the world, and their failure riches for the Gentiles, how much more their fullness!* (Romans 11:11-12)

What a great reason to pray and be part of the revival of Israel—so that the fullness of what God has for the nations and our ministries comes to pass. Paul clearly explains in Romans that God's plan is to show Israel mercy once again, just as He has shown mercy to the Church, which also has been disobedient. God wants to create *"one new man"* (Eph. 2:15), Jew and Gentile as one in Him. When that happens, I believe it will unleash an avalanche and worldwide wave of glory that we have yet to see! Let it begin today in your life and ministry.

In the Book of Ezekiel, there is mention of a valley of dry bones coming back together and then being raised from the dead. Many use this passage to preach to the Church about arising out of its slumber and lukewarmness; but I believe this passage is actually referring to Israel today. It can be applied to the Church after it has been properly applied first to Israel, to whom it was originally written.

> *So I prophesied as He commanded me, and breath came into them, and they lived, and stood upon their feet, an exceedingly great army. Then He said to me, "Son of man, these bones are the whole house of Israel. They indeed say, 'Our bones are dry, our hope is lost, and we ourselves are cut off!'"* (Ezekiel 37:10-11)

This is clearly a picture of the Jewish people, *"the whole house of Israel,"* who had no homeland and had been scattered and lost. But God is beginning to resurrect and gather His chosen. In 1948 the nation of Israel was re-established and is now in the middle of world events. It is evident that Israel, God's chosen, is a vital link to the future of the nations. The Hebrew language has also been resurrected after 1,700 years.

How does all this relate to moving in resurrection power? The resurrection of Israel and her revival will unleash the last great worldwide harvest of souls and bring resurrection glory back to believers. As we accept and participate in what God is doing for His chosen people, the entire body of believers in Jesus will reap the same resurrection glory that is occurring with Israel as a nation.

> *Therefore prophesy and say to them, "Thus says the Lord God: 'Behold, O My people, I will open your graves and cause you to come up from your graves, and bring you back into the land of Israel. Then you shall know that I am the Lord, when I have*

opened your graves, O My people, and brought you up from
your graves. I will put My Spirit in you and you shall live,
and I will place you in your own land. Then you shall know
that I, the Lord, have spoken it and performed it," says the Lord
(Ezekiel 37:12-14).

Wow, what an exciting time we live in! The Bible says that God is opening His people's graves and bringing them back to their land Israel. This is already beginning to happen; many Jews are moving to Israel, but there are many more who want and need to go home to Israel. Ezekiel commanded the bones to come together; flesh came on them but there was no spirit or breath in them. I believe that as soon as the remnant of God's chosen people goes to Israel, their homeland, God will start to breathe His Spirit upon them and bring national revival. This will in turn cause global revival.

Many from the United States and Western Europe, where the majority of Jews reside today, are moving back to Israel. As you pray them home, help them with their move to Israel, support ministries that help them, reach out to them in Israel and at home, and stand up for them in their time of persecution, and you too will partake of the greatest wave of power, revival, and glory that has ever been experienced.

When we began to bless Israel, our lives and entire ministry changed dramatically. First, we toured Israel—which I recommend all believers do at least once in their lifetime. While on our first trip to Israel in 1994, we were visited in the Upper Room by the Holy Spirit. Also during the trip, my wife and I led 13 Israelis to the Messiah. Having blessed Israel with souls saved and with the outpouring we received in the Upper Room, God rewarded us with nonstop revival for the next five years, which led to a six-month nightly revival with souls saved daily, miracles, and signs.

In 1999, the Lord told us to go again to Israel and to pour out the glory of God, which we were experiencing afresh with demonstrations of power, to the congregations and churches in Israel. We were able to impart what God had given us, and those to whom we ministered began to move in great power, signs, and wonders. Due to this, God told us He would enlarge our ministry because we had deposited His glory into a larger area in Israel. During the next two years, we held large glory/miracle campaigns across Europe, Africa, the United States, and other nations, resulting in many extraordinary miracles and many more salvations. God also opened television opportunities for us, and we were able to purchase our own property and ministry base in Europe to reach the nations on that side of the world, in addition to our U.S. ministry.

In February 2003 we took a team of 50 people to Israel. As we toured and held meetings, Israelis streamed through the doors asking if they could join our singing—they said they felt so happy when they were with us. We rejoiced with them as they rediscovered their Jewish Messiah. During this trip we met with Israeli government officials, blessed them, prayed for them, repented for the Western church's history of anti-Semitism, and resolved to stand with Israel with a declaration signed by many believers abroad. A government official was moved to tears and vowed to give this resolution of support for Israel to the prime minister at the time, Ariel Sharon. This was one of our first steps in reconnecting with Israel, returning to our roots, and standing with the nation of Israel in her time of need.

I believe that in this next, and maybe final move of God, any ministry or believer who does not have some type of emphasis on blessing, praying for, sharing the Messiah, or loving Israel and the Jewish people in these last days, will begin to notice a dwindling of influence and lose their anointing, favor, and finances. For those who don't connect, death and stagnation will occur as we enter the third day— the hour God wants us to return to our early church roots and the first few hundred years of its greatest glory. This reconnection is a major aspect of the *Elijah glory* in these last days; it is restoring our foundation on which we stand as He restores the spirit of Elijah, turning the hearts of the children to the fathers and the fathers to the children.

Pray for the peace of Jerusalem: "May they prosper who love you. Peace be within your walls, prosperity within your palaces." For the sake of my brethren and companions, I will now say, "Peace be within you." Because of the house of the Lord our God, I will seek your good (Psalm 122:6-9).

CHAPTER TEN

ELISHA GLORY

*And so it was, when they had crossed over, that Elijah
said to Elisha, "Ask! What may I do for you, before I am
taken away from you?" Elisha said, "Please let a double
portion of your spirit be upon me" (2 Kings 2:9).*

Elisha wanted to be just like his spiritual father Elijah. That is the
reason he asked for a double portion. Elisha wanted to continue
the legacy, so Elijah, in a sense, would live on through the same glory,
yet stronger. It is recorded that Elijah performed 7 major miracles—
Elisha is credited with 16; the last one was after his death. His bones
so held the glory and sound waves of power that when a dead man was
thrown onto Elisha's bones in the same grave, the man was instantly
resurrected! (See Second Kings 13:21.)

The *Elisha glory* is when the torch of the last generation is passed
to the next generation with even greater power. To operate in this
realm, there are some important principles to understand. Recently,
several spiritual leaders and apostles of the faith have gone on to be
with the Lord—now is the time to walk into the Elisha mantle and
continue where they left off.

To do this, we must be willing to stand with those we consider our
spiritual leaders when they are attacked or criticized. This is the true
test of our love and friendship. When we are close friends to those
leaders who are being promoted, blessed, and honored, it is easy to
want to be part of their company. But the test comes during persecution. The disciples were severely tested. Judas wanted what he could

get from Jesus' popularity. He wanted the same power for miracles, esteem in the eyes of others, and a place in the government next to Jesus when He would, supposedly, overthrow the Roman government. Of course, Judas did not realize that it was the *spiritual* Kingdom of God on the earth that He was implementing at that time. When Judas and the others realized that the fun part was over and Jesus was going to be mocked, scourged, crucified, and humiliated, they had second thoughts about openly demonstrating their association with Jesus. When you know someone and his true heart, it does not matter what someone else says, or what is written that claims otherwise. This will be the place of promotion or demotion depending on our stand in that moment.

This is going to be the model for the true apostolic wave that is coming: believers who are willing to lay down their lives for those whom God has placed them here to serve—ultimately, the Lord Jesus Himself. The disciples left all to follow Jesus and Jesus said to them that such *"will do even greater things than these, because I go to the Father"* (John 14:12 AMP).

That is when the double portion comes, when we receive the spiritual inheritance of our fathers in the faith because we were faithful to serve and honor them. Elisha left all to follow Elijah, a type of Jesus, and he received the *"greater things,"* a double portion anointing—and gave God all the glory.

Few people in our day have really tapped into the double portion of what the Church saw even 50 years ago in regard to the glory, power, and miracles. Why is this? Few today have even the same portion as Kathryn Kuhlman, A.A. Allen, and Jack Coe, just to name a few of the great healing evangelists of the 1950s.

RUTH HEFLIN

I was blessed to know Ruth Heflin, a prophet, apostolic leader, and minister. She was like Elijah in the sense that she was a prophetess unto the Lord like none other I have ever seen. She prophesied and spoke the word of the Lord to more presidents around the world than any other believer. She moved in signs and wonders and often glistened with "glory dust." With one prophecy alone, she would totally turn your world upside down, and the prophecy would already begin happening as she was speaking it. Just being around her, I felt as if my entire walk with God was thrown into a supernatural acceleration that took me years ahead of my time.

She treated my wife and me like family and friends from the first day we met. We ministered with her in her special camp meetings and also received great impartations through her ministry. Yet there was another element that was totally different from the impartations we received over the years. It was the immense love she had for us and for those around her. I knew she loved me as a son, and that made all the difference in the world. When she came under attack and was criticized for the new things or revelation she was having—as she was usually ahead of her time, but in God's perfect timing—we always felt compelled to stand with her and continue to show that she was our mother in the Lord and role model, even if it meant we would receive some of the persecution. Sometimes she was very popular and at other times she took a different stand from all the others.

I remember seeing her pray with tears for President Bill Clinton and telling me that he would not be impeached and would be re-elected because God had a plan. It had nothing to do with whether or not he deserved it. God simply told Ruth that it would have adverse effects on the United States, our economy, and the Gospel going out from our shores if he were taken out of office in such a way as it was at that particular time.

One thing was sure: because she prayed for him and many other government officials, she was often invited by the president to come and share the word of the Lord with him. Many other presidents and dignitaries invited her as well. Doors were open to her because she prayed *for* people, not *against* them. She would not allow her tongue to destroy a person of authority but instead prayed for those in authority despite their beliefs or sin.

We decided to do likewise and to pray for President Clinton to change. We prayed that he would repent publicly on national television. Sometimes you must not go with the crowd if you want to keep that anointing, even when your own reasoning does not understand what is happening. Soon after our prayers, he was on television repenting.

Ruth was used to birth a new revival of the glory of God and signs and wonders. In her camp meetings every imaginable sign and wonder took place, which, of course, ruffled the feathers of those comfortable with the status quo. We again staked our ground and said that we were part of this new wave of God. We saw many souls saved, multitudes healed, and governments open up to us around the world—and the blessings continue to this day.

Ruth became very ill after a car accident and soon she went to be with the Lord. We had been with her just weeks before. In fact, the weekend she died she was scheduled to minister with me in a big conference in The Haag, Holland. I arrived at the conference without Ruth, and the pastor asked me where she was. When I said she had passed away, he told me I would have to speak during her sessions as well as mine. I did not know what to say.

How could I fill her shoes when others were expecting her to speak? The Lord showed me about walking in her shoes and mantle in a greater way. I was to minister in her sessions under her anointing as well as mine. I was to walk into the "double portion," which included the anointing and glory on my own life that I was faithful to as a steward, as well as the inheritance of some of her anointing, grace, and glory. As I ministered the glory, the prophetic, signs and wonders, salvations, and the glory doubled and multiplied like I had never seen before—and that was only the beginning.

During the conference, which ended on a Sunday, the Lord told me to go to Ruth's funeral. The only problem: the funeral was in the United States on Tuesday, and I was returning to France on Monday from Holland to rejoin my wife and kids, who were awaiting my return. I told the Lord how hard it would be to leave Holland by Monday, take a train to France, and then find a plane ticket at the last minute on the same day. I explained to the Lord that I had just been with Ruth a few weeks before. The Lord told me that I had to see her off until the end, just as Elisha stayed with Elijah until the end and received the double portion. The Lord impressed upon me that it was of the utmost importance that I go, no matter what the cost.

I quickly called the airlines and miraculously found a ticket. I rushed to France, grabbed my wife, and we rushed to the airport, where we almost missed our flight. That night upon arriving in the United States, I went to Ashland, Virginia, where her body had lain the night before the funeral. As we walked into the room, the glory was so thick that we began to weep—not just because she had passed away, but because of the intense glory that filled the room. It was stronger than when she was alive. I asked the Lord how this could be. Then He explained to me the passage when even the bones of Elisha had raised a man from the dead. The glory was so strong on his dead physical body that a dead man was raised simply by touching it. (See Second Kings 13:21.)

The Lord told me to touch her body and a double portion would be imparted. As she was now in a higher realm of glory in Heaven, her body was the point of contact to transmit the glory between Heaven and earth. As we laid our hands upon her body, the power of God shot though us like an electrical surge that can only be explained as *resurrection glory*. Little did we know that we would soon be sitting next to our new *glory friends*, Mahesh and Bonnie Chavda. They also had received a mighty impartation and inheritance from Ruth. This was another reason God sent us to the funeral—so He could direct us to our next covenant relationship in His glory. Since then, we have seen a much greater glory and definitely at least a double portion of what we had before this trip.

THE MASTER KEY TO THE DOUBLE PORTION

I have noticed something important about those who walk with the greatest mantles—they also honor Israel and the Jewish people, who are the spiritual parents of all believers—the Church.

As mentioned previously, as we honor our spiritual parents, Israel and the Jewish people, God promises a special blessing. In fact, in these last days those who do not honor Israel will not receive the double portion. In Malachi, the spirit of Elijah being restored is connected to the hearts of the fathers (Israel) turning to their children, and the children (the Church) to their fathers. How can we receive a double portion of what the early church had if we don't identify, honor, and associate ourselves with our spiritual fathers and their off-spring today? It will require us to stand firm with Israel in her time of crises when it is not popular to do so.

Ministries that are sincerely praying, fasting, and interceding for our spiritual parents, Israel and the Jews, who birthed us into the faith, will experience a whole new dimension in God. God is also calling many to support the work of God in Israel and to identify with them.

> *Many of the people of Israel are now enemies of the Good News, and this benefits you Gentiles. Yet they are still the people He loves because He chose their ancestors Abraham, Isaac, and Jacob. For God's gifts and His call can never be withdrawn* (Romans 11:28-29 NLT).

We see a generational blessing that doubles and multiplies. Abraham, blessed by God, left a spiritual inheritance to his son, Isaac. Isaac was born with an already-blessed status left from his father; plus, whatever else he would do for God would be added and doubled. Each generation that honored its fathers received an even greater blessing. Jacob received the blessings of Abraham and that of his own father Isaac, plus whatever else he would be and do for God.

If we cut ourselves off from identifying with the Jewish people, we lose that generational blessing and are cut off from the root of where the blessings began. The blessings came out of Abraham and the Jewish people. As we re-plug ourselves into that root, we tap into all the blessings from Abraham all the way to Jesus, the early church, and today. Take a strong stand with your forefather Israel and see the inheritance and double portion come upon you. Incorporate intercession for Israel and the Jewish people around the world, for their salvation, protection, and their return to the land of their forefathers.

JUDEO-CHRISTIAN HERITAGE

Esther is a type of the Church. She had a good position in life and had favor with the king. The Church is often in this place, especially in the West. We are living off of the blessings that our forefathers, Israel and the Jewish apostles, laid for us. Many of us are comfortable, and things are going fairly well. But there is a problem. The king knows not that Esther is a Jew, and now there is an extermination decree. She is in a desperate position. Will she go before the king and risk losing her position, esteem, prosperity, and even her life by identifying herself with the Jews? It was known in Esther's day that anyone who went before the king without permission could be executed. Furthermore, how would the king respond to her request to annul the declaration to kill the entire Jewish race?

She had two options. She could stay and do nothing and continue receiving the benefits of a queen; or she could do something about it. Mordecai told her that she was born, blessed, and honored in her present position for a purpose, *"And who knows but that you have come to royal position for such a time as this?"* (Esther 4:14n NIV)

In other words, the only reason God blessed and favored her in such a way was so she could use this favor to bless Israel. If she failed, she would have missed the reason for her existence, blessed to be a blessing to Israel. She chose to reveal her true identity to the king. We, too, must reveal our true identity as children of God and offspring of Israel. Will we be silent in these days when it is unpopular to stand with Israel and the Jewish people; or will we reveal that we are one with Israel, and honor our spiritual fathers of the faith and Jesus Himself, who came as a Jew?

The United States and Europe are facing this same dilemma. The nations that have experienced great revival in Christendom are among the most blessed and respected nations in the world. Will America and her allies stand by Israel and the Jews, knowing that their blessings originated when they helped Israel become a nation again and became a refuge for many Jews? Or will we close our eyes and try to be politically correct so as to possibly avoid future enemy attacks? If we don't take a strong stand with that which initiated our blessing, we will eventually lose what we are trying to save. We must once again stand with the root of our blessing and spiritual inheritance instead of cutting off our root system in hopes of self-preservation.

And if some of the branches were broken off, and you, being a wild olive tree, were grafted in among them, and with them became a partaker of the root and fatness of the olive tree, do not boast against the branches. But if you do boast, remember that you do not support the root, but the root supports you (Romans 11:17-18).

Joseph had a testing similar to that of today's Western nations. Although a Jew, he became great in the Gentile nation of Egypt. He used his favored position not just for himself but also to save Israel from starvation. He revealed his true identity and his association with his brothers and Israel. Moses did the same and chose to suffer affliction with God's people rather than to enjoy the pleasures of sin in the house of Pharaoh (see Heb. 11:24-25). Receiving the double portion of God's glory and anointing rests heavily upon this principle of revealing your identity and standing with God's chosen people.

Ruth followed Naomi, her Jewish mother-in-law, and God blessed her for it. She identified herself with Naomi and told her, "...*Wherever you go, I will go...your people shall be my people, and your God, my God*" (Ruth 1:16). That is what you call identifying with Israel. She was a Gentile, yet followed and identified with her Jewish mother-in-law. She eventually met Boaz, who was to be her husband, and who is a type of Christ. Boaz gave her a double portion of the grain that others were receiving when he heard about her sacrifice and love for her mother-in-law. Ruth is even in the family lineage of Jesus. We, too, will reap a double-portion *Elisha anointing* of everything that God has planned to give us if we honor our spiritual father, Israel in these last days, and use our favor, finances, gifts, and anointing to bless Israel and prepare her to accept her Messiah.

Cornelius was a Gentile who supported Israel. God blessed him spiritually when Peter came to his house and brought salvation and an outpouring of the Holy Spirit. Cornelius and his household became the first Gentile converts. (See Acts 10.) This Roman centurion was said to love the Jewish people, and even had helped build their synagogue.

When Jesus learned how Cornelius helped the Jewish people, He was drawn to bless him: He answered his prayers (see Acts 10:4).

THE DOUBLE PORTION AND THE FIRSTBORN

Tradition demanded that the firstborn son receive a double portion of the inheritance and blessing of the father. That is why Esau and Jacob fought for the birthright from their birth to the time that Esau sold his birthright—though he regretted it later (see Gen. 25:26; Heb. 12:17). I believe the Lord is about to release a firstborn double portion now to those who are attentive and seeking it.

The firstborn into the Kingdom were the Jews. From the Old Testament and in the New, they were the first to receive the commandments, to be called His people, to receive salvation and the baptism of the Holy Spirit. As they are the firstborn, God promises blessings for them. In Isaiah chapters 60 to 62, the prophet speaks of the restoration of Israel and the Jews to their land and to their God.

> *And they shall rebuild the old ruins, they shall raise up the former desolations, and they shall repair the ruined cities, the desolations of many generations. Strangers shall stand and feed your flocks, and the sons of the foreigner shall be your plowmen and your vinedressers* (Isaiah 61:4-5).

Here we see what is already coming to pass in our day, as the Jewish people have begun to return and restore the nation that was practically in ruins. Verse 7 gets more exciting!

> *Instead of your shame you shall have double honor, and instead of confusion they shall rejoice in their portion. Therefore in their land they shall possess double; everlasting joy shall be theirs* (Isaiah 61:7).

God promises a double portion to the Jewish people above all the other nations and people of the earth. If we identify with them as Ruth did with Naomi, we too will receive a double portion and fully enter into the *Elisha anointing!* If we fully identify ourselves with the Jews and Israel and make it known that we are of the same family, whether it produces blessing or persecutions, we are saying that we are joined with the firstborn. I believe that if we look at Israel as if it is also our land—at least spiritually—and if we intercede and fast and pray for the Jews around the world to know the Messiah, we will also be considered by God as the firstborn.

Jacob disguised himself as his older brother, Esau, to receive first-born status and blessing from his blind father. Because his father could not tell the difference, since he smelled, felt, and almost talked like his brother, he gave Jacob the blessing. We must identify with the firstborn and God's purposes in the earth for them so much so that we become mistaken for being the firstborn, and we will receive a double portion.

But, if we make a distinction between "us and them," we will miss the double-portion blessing. If we say we are the Church and we are now the beloved apple of God's eye apart from Israel and the Jews, then we will lose our portion. God is now *restoring* all things, not dividing. God is preparing the *"one new man"* by taking the Ruths and the Naomis and joining those two into one—producing the double portion! Identify yourself as coming from the same family and lineage as Israel through Jesus and pray for their salvation; and you will begin to enter into the double portion.

Those who watch and pray for Jerusalem, and spiritually as well as physically help to rebuild her ruins, will receive double-portion glory.

> *Because I love Zion, I will not keep still. Because my heart yearns for Jerusalem, I cannot remain silent. I will not stop praying for her until her righteousness shines like the dawn, and her salvation blazes like a burning torch* (Isaiah 62:1 NLT).

> *O Jerusalem, I have posted watchmen on your walls; they will pray day and night, continually. Take no rest, all you who pray to the Lord. Give the Lord no rest until He completes His work, until He makes Jerusalem the pride of the earth* (Isaiah 62:6-7 NLT).

MIND, THOUGHTS, AND GLORY

CHAPTER ELEVEN

YOUR THOUGHTS

Nothing can stop the man with the right mental attitude from achieving his goal; nothing on earth can help the man with the wrong mental attitude.
—Thomas Jefferson

As [a man] *thinks in his heart, so is he.*
—King Solomon (Proverbs 23:7)

Stepping a little closer to glory means realizing how important your thoughts are. Just as you are what you eat, you also are what you think. The way you see yourself is who you become. Every action is based first on a thought. Once your thoughts start to change—about yourself, God, and life—your life starts to change. Because actions are the results of thoughts, to see change you need to allow your thoughts to be conditioned in a way that will bring you maximum results in every area of your life. You need to take control of your thoughts and not allow just any thoughts to dominate your life. That's why it's key to renew your mind. Just as raw food has an energy force, thoughts are so powerful that they release energy—good or bad—depending on the thoughts.

When you get a strange dream of someone chasing you or trying to hurt you, your heart beats faster and you wake up feeling exhausted, as if it really happened. Your mind treated it as fact.

When you watch an intense, action-filled movie, your mind sends the same signals to your body as if you were in the car on the high-speed chase; this causes reactions in your stress levels, heartbeat, and so on. Your body does not differentiate between whether what you are seeing is reality or simply a movie or dream. As you see the images in your mind or on a screen, your body reacts to them positively or negatively.

Thoughts are creative in nature, and if thoughts are consistent enough, they start to manifest into reality. The more you think and focus on a particular thing, the more it will become a reality.

When you start to think about something negative, like how you will pay your bills, or if you will get evicted from your home, or lose your job, your body suddenly starts to release toxins into your bloodstream that affect your heart rate, arteries, energy, immune system, and many other things. Thoughts of anger, rejection, fear, or bitterness all produce negative effects on your body and your peace and joy—releasing dangerous toxins into your body. Just *thinking* about certain negative things can adversely affect your life and your health.

Negative thoughts put you in a downward spiral; and when so much energy is devoted to these thoughts, you can at times feel too worn out and depleted to think and act on positive thoughts that build you up and drive you to achievement, solutions, and supernatural health. When people too often think negative thoughts, others can sense that, and it drains them as well. People tend to distance themselves from those who speak, think, and act negatively. When people live in a constant state of fear and anxiety, this depletes the immune system. Such people get sick much faster than those who don't live and think this way.

Start to think on things that are helpful, exciting, positive, and energizing!

Finally, brethren, whatever things are true, whatever things are noble, whatever things are just, whatever things are pure, whatever things are lovely, whatever things are of good report,

if there is any virtue and if there is anything praiseworthy—
meditate on these things (Philippians 4:8).

VISUALIZATION

When you see yourself as achieving great health and joy, thinking the best of people, and having other positive thoughts, this releases a rejuvenation of your cells; your health improves. If you start to see yourself in great internal and external shape, your mind will send a signal to your body helping you to achieve this or any other goal.

Just as there are laws of gravity and laws pertaining to flying (airplanes), there are also laws that affect the natural and spiritual realms. "*As* [a man] *thinks in his heart, so is he*" (Prov. 23:7) was written by the great man of wisdom, King Solomon. Thinking you are more than able to attain supernatural health or weight loss causes you to achieve it. If you think there is no way, then that is what you will get. Many sicknesses are a result of wrong thinking that leads to wrong actions about food choices, or emotional patterns that results in sickness.

You need to take full control of what you allow to enter your mind. If it is a negative thought, quickly replace it with a positive thought of someone who told you he or she loved you, or when your baby was born, or anything positive that happened in your life. You have to take negative thoughts captive and then send them on their way.

Everything you see around you was first created in someone's mind, and then came into manifested reality. You are what you think about and how you see yourself.

OVERCOMING PAST THOUGHTS

How do you get rid of negative thoughts that have been there since youth? Many people have been conditioned as kids because of negative thoughts from parents, teachers, and other authority figures in their lives—even other classmates.

Maybe your father told you that you would never succeed or did not show the love you needed at the time. You might have been picked on in school. Because this might have been etched into your mind at a very young age, it affected all your decisions or indecision—affecting your relationships and life. Oftentimes later in life, people discover they have hidden anger or resentment against those they blame for their present lives.

To start changing, you have to first take charge of your life and not let someone else dictate who you were really created to be. The most powerful force in the world is to forgive the person who hurt you in the past so that you can go on and create a new future. Continuing to hold on to what someone said or did, as bad as it was at the time, will only limit you and continue to be self-destructive. If you hold on to it, then they win and you will become what people told you that you were.

But if you let go and forgive, you will win and prove to be totally opposite of what was spoken over you as a curse. When you forgive them, it will feel like a million pounds of weight lifted off of you— freeing you from a prison of defeat into a new life of limitless possibilities. Also, the original culprits, who may have had a hidden or a subconscious sense of guilt about how they treated you, may even sense a new freedom as they feel the release. Try it right now—simply say, *"I forgive so-and-so for what he or she did or said to me."* Say it several times to imprint it into your psyche and spirit.

Now you are on your way to supernatural health. This is the most powerful thing you could ever do! You will notice a new joy, and people will become attracted to you and the love in you from God because of this new sense of love and forgiveness exuding from you.

ASSOCIATIONS

If you hang around people who always put you down and are always cynical, critical, or depressed, and they don't want to change, you need to make some new friends who propel you toward who you want to be. Guilt by association is real. You take on the positive or negative attributes of those with whom you spend time. When you hang around with angry people, you tend to be angry, as anger slowly but surely creeps upon you as you tolerate it.

Make no friendship with an angry man, and with a furious man do not go, lest you learn his ways and set a snare for your soul (Proverbs 22:24-25).

FOCUS

Focus on things that are noble and positive. This Scripture from Philippians is worthy of repeating:

And now, dear brothers and sisters, one final thing. Fix your thoughts on what is true, and honorable, and right, and pure, and lovely, and admirable. Think about things that are excellent and worthy of praise (Philippians 4:8 NLT).

You always move toward what you focus on. Focus on how you will feel when you achieve this or that dream or goal. Once you start to imagine how you feel, you actually start to tap into the future, living the feelings of joy and satisfaction of a future event before it happens. Your mind and body can't always tell if what you are thinking is in the present or future. But simply start now to cause your body, spirit, and everything else to react positively according to what you are thinking—whether it be present, future, or past.

As you strongly focus more on what you are aiming for, your brain will start to work overtime to find the solution in your subconscious while you sleep. Also, help from above, from the Creator, will start to flow, as you are in tune with the patterns and laws that govern how things operate in the invisible world.

Your mind is like a computer chip that has only so much memory or capacity. If your mind is overly focused on a negative problem—constantly worried about what may happen—your thoughts may be overloaded with fear. Even if the solution were to be downloaded to you, there would not be any more room in the memory bank of your mind to receive the message. If the message box on your answering machine is full, you cannot receive the important, life-changing message you are waiting for from above. Clear your mind of fear and worry, so that you can make room for the solutions that will come to you when you create the proper environment to receive them.

DESIRE

What you think about often leads to stronger desires. When you couple consistent thinking and desire, they start to manifest into reality. The stronger your desire, the faster you will act on it. Again, it all starts with thoughts. If you casually desire to be in good health but are not motivated enough to act on it, then your desire needs to be increased to spur you to action—just like when you strongly desired chocolate chip cookies because of a commercial you kept seeing over and over. The result is the same: you run to the store and buy them— or you start eating better and exercising.

If you start to think thoughts about what you want to achieve or you see yourself 30 pounds lighter, eventually you will act in accordance with those thoughts. Again, as mentioned earlier, thoughts and visuals have an effect on the body, mind, and spirit. When you dream while sleeping, your body and mind do not always know the difference between what is a present reality or a future-tense scenario that you may be catching a glimpse of. The same thing works when watching television or a movie. Your heart can still race during an intense scene even though it's not occurring in actuality. Even a mental picture that you imagine in your brain can start working for you or against you.

See your future and destiny and think of these things even now and on a consistent basis, and you will start to attract the necessities, connections, and resources for a fulfilling life.

SPEECH

What you speak has an amazing effect on everything you do and on your body. Speech is so powerful that it is recorded that everything was created by it. In the beginning, the Creator spoke, *"Let there be light:' and there was light"* (Gen. 1:3)

Speech and sounds, though invisible to the naked eye, are real objects. If an opera singer can sing at a high pitch and break glass, then it is a tiny object—like a pebble—but smaller. At high speeds or frequencies, it can pierce through another object. Scientists call these "sound waves."

Sound waves created by speech are so small that if you were to divide the smallest particles and atoms into some of the smallest forms inside them, at their core you would find vibrating sound waves called quarks. These sound waves are embedded in everything on the earth, including rocks, food, trees, and everything ever created. This means that speech was one of the first ingredients that created everything else you see and the invisible things you don't see. This also means that these sounds waves can be altered and respond to other sound waves or speech.

Albert Einstein's theory of relativity explains it well, as he was way ahead of his time. As previously mentioned, his theory, in simplified terms, defines E as energy, and M as matter or substance. Basically, Einstein concluded that energy is real and is considered matter even though it is invisible to the naked eye. You cannot see electricity, but you know it is real when you turn on a light and see its effect.

Likewise, thoughts and speech release energy. So when you think and speak certain things, you are actually releasing matter or creating things—good or bad.

SOUND WAVES

In certain studies done on water particles, the water particles responded to how the scientists spoke to them. As mentioned in my book, *Natural to Super Natural Health,* in studies conducted by Japanese researcher Masaru Emoto, water particles and other subatomic particles actually respond to sound and even speech or words spoken to them. If this is true, then every created thing can hear in a sense and respond in some way, as they were first created with the same core ingredients—sound and light.

In some nations, such as Canada, where it is legal, doctors use a procedure called high-intensity focused ultrasound—high-energy sound waves—to destroy cancer cells. These are sound waves; but imagine the power of speech against sickness, especially if you use the highest power source, the Creator's power and the name of the Messiah Yeshua, when commanding objects such as disease to vanish.

Start to speak the things you want to see manifested in your life. If you are going for a job interview, say that you are going to have great favor with everyone you meet, and you will be successful. Start telling your body that it is strong and healthy and that no sickness can survive in such a healthy state. Sometimes I will even say with great joy and humor that my body is so healthy that sickness does not feel comfortable around me and just has to leave. Actually, even quantum physics, science, spiritual giants, and the ancients all confirm the power of speech.

Create your day—each morning—by speaking what you believe will be created, that you will be successful in all that you do, that you are full of energy, and that you will have favor with everyone you meet after connecting first to the Creator's power and love through the Messiah. This will cause things to shift from the invisible realm to the visible realm and will also take you from natural to supernatural health. Your health will be determined, in large part, by how well you control and bridle your speech to create health and life.

Death and life are in the power of the tongue, and those who love it will eat its fruit (Proverbs 18:21).

FOOD AFFECTS THOUGHTS

When your daily diet consists mostly of eating foods that are not natural, the dead foods that you eat that are not energy foods will start to drain you and make you feel less energized. This feeling of being drained leads to grouchiness, negative thoughts, and complaints. So what you eat *does* affect your thoughts eventually. And your thoughts affect what you eat.

For instance, a lack of an amino acid called tryptophan can lead to depression. Tryptophan is found in foods such as turkey. That is why people feel a sense of contentment and are relaxed after the large Thanksgiving turkey meal. Salmon, tuna, and lamb also contain tryptophan. Even better are raw, high-protein foods such as spinach, kale, broccoli, goji berries, spirulina, chlorella, blue-green algae, and other raw foods, many of which can be found at any health food store or in tablet form at www.sedonanaturals.com. Through cooking, trypto-phan is destroyed, as it is sensitive to heat. Meats contain this amino acid, but if you eat only cooked meat and potatoes (a bad combination for digestion), the amino acid is destroyed. Start incorporating lots of raw foods into your diet and see the difference it makes! For more information on healthy eating and a healthier lifestyle, which can affect you mentally, emotionally, and spiritually, read my book, *Natural to Super Natural Health*.

When your thoughts are in order, and your physical body and spiritual life are in good shape and working in sync, you are then ready to accept your God-given future as He has designed it for you. You are now capable of co-creating your future in God by speaking, thinking, desiring, praying and acting on what you know your destiny is!

CHAPTER TWELVE

CREATING YOUR FUTURE

If you can imagine it, you can achieve it; if you
can dream it, you can become it.
—William Arthur Ward

The invisible world is more real than we think. In fact, it determines what occurs in our visible world. Recent studies in quantum physics have discovered that subatomic particles will begin to change form simply by being observed by humans. As in the case with water particles when they were spoken to in a certain way, they change form according to angry words, love, or other words connected with a certain emotion.

Everything created on this earth is made up of core subatomic particles that can be altered by human observation—amazing! Just thinking about certain things immediately causes either a positive or negative effect on your body, whether it is angry thoughts releasing poisons or happy, loving thoughts releasing healing.

If this is true, then objects in the invisible world can change or be re-created by simply being observed or even thought about. By observing something that is in your future and looking and thinking about it, invisible subatomic particles start to shift, causing things to come your way as they shift from what is potential to reality. Whatever you think about and speak starts to be created.

When you get a creative idea or inspiration and start to think about it more intensely, it is already being created. Then when you start to speak and declare that you will do this or that, the reality of it starts to speed up even faster toward fulfillment; and soon after, action follows on your behalf. Before you know it, you run into someone or get a phone call that is the open door into the very thing that started as a download into your brain—a creative thought from the Creator. You become what you think and speak about.

It is even recorded in the Book of Genesis that the Creator spoke and then things were created. This makes more sense today, given the scientific language and discoveries that explain how this could be possible.

YOUR BRAIN IS A RADIO TRANSMITTER

Many do not realize that the human brain acts like a radio transmitter sending out frequencies. Have you ever thought about someone you needed to call for a few days, and suddenly he (or she) called you and said he had been thinking of you for the past three days? When the intensity of thought is strong enough, it sends a signal to other brains. Everything is made of atoms—protons, neutrons, electrons, and frequencies—including thought and speech.

If an opera singer can sing and release invisible sounds waves at a certain pitch that breaks glass, so can a strong enough thought create subatomic particles in the form of frequencies.

I once heard that an experiment was conducted to prove this point. Every object has a certain frequency coming out of it. In one experiment researchers aimed radio frequencies at a bar of gold. When they measured the frequency of the gold bar, they discovered that the vibration and frequency of the gold changed when a radio wave or x-ray was aimed at it. Next they experimented with a person intensely aiming his thoughts on a gold bar. What they discovered was that after the thoughts were aimed at the gold bar, the vibration and frequency emitting from the gold bar was equally changed due to the strong thought frequency aimed at it from the brain.

Thoughts can send out a weak signal or a strong signal. Have you ever suddenly been hit with a very heavy, dark, sad feeling and wondered why, as there was no natural situation that would have caused you to feel that way? Then shortly afterward, did you discover that someone was very upset with you and was not only intensely thinking thoughts about you but also was speaking negatively about you? Now you know why you felt that way. The reverse also occurs; you may feel a sense of excitement, as if something really good is about to happen, but you don't know why or what. A few days later, you realize that a decision had been made on your behalf that was very favorable for you. You already received the frequency being transmitted days before actual reality hit you.

Our brains transmit energy on different frequencies. You can transmit with as much power as you choose. When your brain transmits frequencies through your thoughts, it is picked up by other brains that have the ability to pick up such signals.

What you think about also affects physical matter. I heard a story of a doctor who mixed up the test results of two patients. One patient had full-blown cancer and had three months to live. The other patient's tests showed he was cancer-free. The doctor accidentally switched the results. When the man who was cancer-free was told he had three months to live, immediately his brain began to send very strong signals that indeed there was a cancer in his body. He thought about it day and night; his emotions believed it and his actions confirmed it as he planned his funeral. Within three months he actually developed terminal cancer and died.

The other man who actually had the cancer was mistakenly told that he did not have cancer. His brain began to send signals of healing. He started to dream again of all the things in life he wanted to accomplish. He canceled his funeral plans and began to be thankful that he was healed and was a better person for it, thanking the Creator that he was given a second chance. When he was checked again three months later, the cancer had gone into remission and he was cancer-free. Both these patients' brains released very powerful, intense, radio-type frequencies that in turn created responses and signals in their bodies.

Just thinking about something that makes you angry, sad, or negative can get your immune system to start shutting down; your heart starts to beat faster, your blood rushes to your face, and negative toxins are released into your bloodstream, clogging you up—just from toxic thoughts of anger, resentment, bitterness, rejection, and the like. It's not that you will never experience these thoughts, but how fast you dispose of them is the key to good mental, physical, and spiritual health.

One rule of thumb is never to go to bed in this state of mind. Release it before you sleep so that it does not get into your system all through the night. Ephesians 4:26 says, *"'Be angry, and do not sin'; do not let the sun go down on your wrath."*

The best approach is to simply say out loud, "I release this situation and I release and forgive that person." Next, discipline your mouth not to speak about it; if you continue speaking about it, your words will recreate the situation, and the thoughts will start to kick in, recreating the past all over again along with the toxic emotions that come with it.

Another interesting concept is that if objects and people can pick up thoughts and words, imagine the power of thoughts and words if a person is in meditation or prayer and connected to the Creator. Then imagine the power of those words compared to someone not connected to a higher power.

Throughout history, the words of certain people carried much greater power than those of the average person, to the point where people were spellbound when they spoke. Some of the most famous people in history had such power when they spoke because their words were backed up by very intense thought frequencies. These in turn were backed up by a powerful spiritual force they received in personal times of reflection or meditation, despite hard times. These are the words and phrases that today are used in everyday language; they once were coined by people who knew the power of thoughts and words. Thoughts and words, if used correctly, can create situations that did not otherwise exist. One example of this was when President Ronald Reagan spoke at the Berlin Wall and uttered, "Tear down this wall!" His advisors told him those words should not be spoken but he did it anyway. It is said that he was also a man of prayer. Shortly afterward, the Berlin Wall was torn down.

Winston Churchill was another powerful speaker. At the most critical time of World War II, in his speech Churchill had to describe a great military disaster Great Britain had just suffered, and warn of a possible Nazi German invasion attempt, without casting doubt on eventual victory. His speech shifted people's minds and hearts from probable defeat when all odds were against them to a hope for victory. The following words he spoke shifted Heaven and earth in his and the Allies' favor:

> We have before us an ordeal of the most grievous kind. We have before us many, many long months of struggle and of suffering. You ask, what is our policy? I will say: It is to wage war, by sea, land, and air, with all our might and with all the strength that God can give us; to wage war against a monstrous tyranny never surpassed in the dark, lamentable catalogue of human crime. That is our policy. You ask, what is our aim? I can answer in one word: It is victory, victory at all costs, victory in spite of all terror, victory, however long and hard the road may be.

WORDS THAT CREATE

When your goals and destiny are observed and thought about consistently, the invisible framework starts to create circumstances for these things to become reality. Now it's time to kick it into turbo mode! Words that are spoken with absolute belief, faith, and certainty will bring unity of focus and create those things.

If, for example, you casually say, "I will become an A-list actor" but your thoughts and beliefs are not congruent with what you just said or believe, this causes imbalance and hinders the visible manifestation. Others might say, "I will lose 30 pounds by this date and be in the best shape possible, and nothing will stop me!" If they speak with total conviction and passion, and clearly visualize themselves thinner and healthier, then they are going to see it happen as they will act on it. You have to incorporate all of yourself—words, thoughts, passion, and emotions—at a higher level; then working together in unison, those attributes will result in breakthroughs in any area of life.

When you speak something that you intend to become reality, what percentage of power is in those words? Are your mind, body, passion, and focus 100 percent behind your words? Or are you speaking with maybe only 10 percent intensity of belief, thoughts, and conviction? To the degree that your mind, emotions, thoughts, will, passion, and words are all congruent at the same high level of intensity, this determines the speed and probability of what you are speaking to occur. Basically, if you can unite your mind, body, will, emotions, and actions on a high level of energy and focus, there is not much that can stop the thing you are aiming for from becoming reality. Even when we worship God, He asks us to worship not just with our lips but using our heart, soul (mind, will, emotions), and strength. Deuteronomy 6:5 says: *"Love the Lord your God with all your heart, with all your soul, and with all your strength."*

PASSION

When you are totally passionate about something that you feel or know you are supposed to do or become, things will start to come your way. The level of emotion and intensity or drive is a huge determining factor in seeing it come to reality. You have to want something badly enough to do something about it.

Action on your part to cooperate with your vision or destiny usually does not come without an intense internal force called passion. For some people, it's getting a report from a doctor that they have cancer or some other sickness that serves as a driving force to change their lifestyle. To others it's not so much a negative that drives them, but a glimpse into the future of the joy they will feel when they are lighter, thinner, and more energetic. That joy of who they can become starts to increase their passion and drive!

You can go through all the steps mechanically and still miss the mark if there is not a sense of excitement, drive, and passion in whatever you undertake to accomplish. If you could do anything in life and money was not an object, what would you do? Start to work toward that thing in life that naturally drives you, and you will accomplish so much more than trying to do things that others expect of you, which do not necessarily motivate you. This is a huge secret to success—finding your purpose in life, with passion.

Everything produces itself after its own kind. Apple seeds produce apples; orange seeds produce oranges; and so on since the beginning of time. You have natural talents and abilities that you were born with. Start to use those gifts and talents to help others and you will have a great sense of fulfillment. This will also draw you closer to the Creator. So many people just exist and do not passionately live life to the fullest. They have not tapped into what they are destined to do or realized their natural talents, gifts, and desires; the world is waiting for their release.

BLOCKAGES

Often we associate a certain goal with pain and suffering. Maybe the last time you were on a diet or tried to exercise, something went wrong and you ended up gaining more weight or hurting yourself at the gym. Then a book like this comes along to really help you, but you have mental and emotional memories of past experiences that block you from taking action. Your conscious mind is saying, "Yes—wow, this is great!" But by the time you are about to take action, all the fears and blockages hinder your progress because of the associations with past failure.

You have to reprogram your mind and body. You can do this by starting to associate change with pleasure, imagining how good you will feel and look—not by what happened last time you tried something new. Also, program your mind by reminding yourself of all the sicknesses you will avoid by starting on this new supernatural health lifestyle. The same is true for anything in life if you can approach it in a positive light that motivates you to action.

When a woman is pregnant or has had lots of pain or complications at childbirth, she may start to say and think, "This is the last time I'm going through this." But then as time goes on and as she is enjoying her new baby, she starts to dream again of the joy and pleasure another child would bring to her, her husband, and her first child. The pain associated with childbirth gets replaced by more positive memories of a new baby as time goes on. This leads to having the faith to overcome the negative programming and lots of positive associations with a second child.

Another example is when someone applies for a new job, or an aspiring actor auditions for a new movie or television show. Sometimes the fear due to a past rejection hinders some from moving on and accomplishing great things. Those who can remove the negative past associations are driven to action by the joy and accomplishment set before them once they are hired. Hebrew 12:2 NIV states, *"Let us fix our eyes on Jesus, the author and perfecter of our faith, who for the joy set before Him endured the cross, scorning its shame, and sat down at the right hand of the throne of God."*

Start to work from the future to the present. Imagine you already have that job, career, book published, healthy, leaner body, and so on. How do you feel now—as if you have already arrived at your greatest dream? As you start to see, imagine, feel, and enjoy right now what in the future you will be feeling, you are actually accelerating its existence—already tapping into the senses you would feel as if it already occurred!

You don't have to wait until the future becomes a reality to actually enjoy the senses and joy of what that will be like. Your body and mind, as I mentioned before, do not know the difference between a future mental image or something occurring now. As you start to see your future and even feel the joy of that goal, you will be tapping into your future *now!* Then all the other details will start to fall into place. You will get more insight on the next step to take, and before you know it, you will become what you already started to think about and enjoy.

The secret is to first define your God-given dream or goal, and then have 100 percent *passion*—get your desire and excitement at full throttle about that dream. Then have 100 percent *belief* that what you are seeing will and is happening and being created; then take 100 percent *action* toward that goal, knowing that it is happening and is out there waiting for you to simply act on it and realize it! Action is where many people stop. You can dream about it and talk about it, but until you finally take action it will be an unrealized dream.

START NOW

Start by taking a baby step right now toward that dream—it may be a phone call, writing the first page of your book, or auditioning for a movie. Or start a business by creating a business plan and even naming it on legalzoom.com as if you already have a business. The rest will fall into place.

As you take your first step, the next step will be clearer as things and the right people and connections start coming your way. Create your future now and bring it into the present by enjoying, celebrating, and seeing yourself already there!

GLORY OF THE NATIONS

Each nation has a particular glory, gift, and treasure that God wants to reveal. The Bible speaks often of the glory and/or wealth of the nations coming to Jerusalem in the last days. (See Isaiah 60:5-9; 66:20 as examples.)

I believe that each nation has a particular and different manifestation and expression of the glory of God. In fact, the fullness of the glory will only be known after every nation on earth experiences revival and discovers her gift manifested in the glory. Then we will see all the glories that God reveals. God has purposely hidden these glories in the nations around the world so that the fullness cannot be experienced by any one nation until all the nations experience a move of God.

When the glory and revival hit Argentina and Africa, mass deliverances were a new expression of the glory that many pastors carried with them to those nations. When the glory hit South Korea, it manifested in a spirit of prayer—so much so that there are now "prayer mountains" all over South Korea, and they have imparted the spirit of persistent prayer to other nations. Australia and New Zealand have manifested the glory of God through a new wave of praise and worship that is sweeping the nations. The Bible says that His praise will come forth from the ends of the earth—we are seeing this happen today.

France has the gift of passion. When believers receive the Lord, they praise, dance, weep and worship, pray and fast, with all their heart. England has produced some of the most renowned Bible teachers in the world with roots from the great revivals of the past. Many other countries are beginning to see new glory invasions. I believe that the Native Americans will see a wave of resurrections from the dead that will be imparted to the nations.

I notice that the more I travel and minister in different nations, the more of God's glory is imparted. Ministries with the most diverse gifts from God and are most open-minded to new things are often ministries whose leaders have traveled to many different countries. They are not focused only on what God is doing now in their own nation, but have seen the glory manifested differently in many nations and have taken it as their own. It is possible to take ownership, in a sense, of a new glory and make it your own. For instance, after we ministered in Africa, there was an immediate increase in mass deliverances whenever the glory would hit our meetings in the United States and Europe.

There are new waves and manifestations of God's glory that have yet to be manifested on the earth. The new glories will only be manifested as nations untouched by God's glory are awakened. The Middle East and Arab nations have not yet seen the awesome glory that will be revealed once God wakes up those sleeping giants. China saw a tremendous glory and reproduced millions of new converts in a short amount of time once the glory invaded that nation. Israel and the world will experience the greatest end-time glory invasion when the King of Glory, the Messiah, comes and takes His place in Jerusalem.

Each nation has a glory that God wants to make known in the earth. In the secular sense, America is known for sports and apple pie, among other things. France is known for perfume and pastry; and Brazil is known for soccer. Now God wants all nations to be known for the glory He will reveal through believers who will stand with Israel and His chosen people.

God is sending people to nations that have never experienced a national move of God. God often sends His people from one nation to another to help that nation dig deep and discover His treasures hidden deep in the soil. Digging may require fasting, prayer, intercession, giving, repentance, and miracles. But after the glory of God is extracted from the ground and starts to surface, the reputation of that nation will change. China was known as a closed Communist country. Now its reputation is changing. Now we hear about China's underground church and the great things God is doing there—despite political and economic changes.

God wants to change the reputation of so-called "bad" nations that are full of "good news" potential. Saul was determined to persecute the church and had earned a bad reputation; but after the glory invasion touched his life and he became Paul, that same determination was transformed into tremendous manifestations of glory that continue to this day to bless the nations.

I believe the ultimate climax of God's glory on the earth will be when Israel rediscovers the glory of God at the return of the Messiah to Jerusalem. The Bible says that we are to *"go into all the world and preach the gospel"* (Mark 16:15) and that *"these signs will follow those who believe"* (Mark 16:17). I believe we have not yet seen all the manifestations of God's glory. The glory will be fully manifested after we go to the nations that have not yet experienced the glory invasion of God in this generation or have never heard the Gospel.

After you leave your country and set foot in another to preach or share the Gospel according to Mark 16:15-18, *"Go into all the world... and these signs will follow"* is activated, and we have full rights to ask God to manifest His glory, leading to many salvations. I believe that churches and believers who cannot go to other nations but will pray and send others with their finances, will also walk in the glory invasion and partake of a greater glory of God in their lives.

As you press into His glory, ask Him to release a *glory invasion of God* in your life and accelerate what He wants to do through you.

40-DAY

GLORY
INVASION
DEVOTIONAL

THE GLORY ZONE

By faith we understand that the worlds were framed by the word of God, so that the things which are seen were not made of things which are visible (Hebrews 11:3).

The writer of Hebrews clearly says that *"things which are seen were not made of things which are visible."* So what are these invisible things that He used to create everything?

The first invisible thing God sent was His own Spirit or Glory upon the earth. Those of us who walk by faith understand that God has His hand in everything. He works behind the scenes to bring about His purposes.

Think about your life and everything "seen" that you have or has happened. Consider that when you live by faith and enter into the glory zone, you can make anything happen. This is how Elijah could command rain to fall or not, and how Ezekiel could command dead, dry human bones to come back together.

First, these men of God immersed themselves in the Spirit or Glory of God, and then they spoke, prophesied, or declared what God told them to speak. Imagine how your life can be different by learning to live like Elijah. Wouldn't you prefer to rule over circumstances instead of having circumstances rule over you?

God says that you can. (See Mark 4:39; John 14:12.)

SOUND WAVES

But Jesus answered, "I tell you, if these become silent,
the stones will cry out!" (Luke 19:40 NASB)

God spoke, and it was created. In fact, everything created was created when God spoke it all into existence. Because of this, there are sound waves imbedded in every created thing.

Creation emits "sound waves of worship" that are invisible to your natural ear, but your spirit receives them. Have you ever noticed that when you alone with nature you often sense the presence of God?

Christ has dominion over all creatures and can do with them as He pleases.

What do you think Jesus meant when He said, "I give you authority and power"? (See Luke 10:19.) How many times has someone tried to give you something, but you refused to accept it? Did you notice that Jesus did not say that He is going to give us authority but rather that He has already given it to us? Have you accepted His gift?

Consider that you already have the power to change your circumstances. Consider that water particles and other subatomic particles actually respond to sound and even to voice recognition. If this is true, then every created thing can hear in a sense and respond in some way; for all things created were first created with the same core ingredients—sound, and the glory or presence of God. That power has been passed to you. What will you do with it?

DAY 3
GLORY INVASION MIRACLES

"O dry bones, hear the word of the Lord!" (Ezekiel 37:4b).

As described in the Creation account in the Book of Genesis, everything was created with sound—the voice of God—directing it to be a certain thing. If you are in the presence of God, it is also possible to redirect an object to become another created thing. One created object can turn into another if directed by sound waves in the form of a command spoken under the direction of the Holy Spirit.

So if we have the faith to see one object turn into another, how much easier is it to see things, once created, able to multiply? Every living thing generally produces after its own kind.

Jesus has given us the authority to command the natural realm. Why then do we act surprised when miracles occur? Jesus chose to accept this reality without question or debate. He never doubted. He just knew what His Father said was the truth and acted on it. When Jesus was told He could do something for someone else, He stepped out, performed miracles daily, and then passed that same gift from God to us.

What is holding you back from stepping out and doing the same?

IF WALLS COULD TALK

For everyone who asks receives, and he who seeks finds,
and to him who knocks it will be opened (Luke 11:10).

We know that everything was created by the glory of God and the sound of His spoken word. So when the heaviness of God's glory is present in a meeting, for example, we know that every body part and creative miracle needed is available. But how do we extract those creative miracles from the glory in the meeting? By realizing that all the miracles and body parts are in the glory—but in an expanded form.

Remember these four dots from the text?

..

..

You can easily see these dots that are placed relatively closely to each other. But imagine if I placed these same four dots in the four corners of a football stadium. You would know they are there, but you would not be able to see them at the same time. Similarly, needed body parts are in the meeting when the glory of God is present. The power is there for miracles, and the body parts are there; now you need to extract a particular body part from the glory realm that is in the room. You do so by declaring the body part to be made manifest and for the parts to come together so you can see the miracle visibly—just as you can see the dots when they are in a compacted form.

Does your church focus on the God of salvation and consequently does it witness many salvations, but not healings? Or does your church emphasize a God who delivers and He manifests as such? God will manifest in the way you perceive Him. Do you limit God? Or do you see Him in unlimited aspects? If so, you will see His unlimited manifestations.

DAY 5
WALKING THROUGH WALLS AND ON WATER

So He said, "Come." And when Peter had come down out of the boat, he walked on the water to go to Jesus (Matthew 14:29).

When you are experiencing extreme glory, you are, in essence, in an expanded glory where the cellular structure of your body may expand. Jesus went through a lot—He was resurrected, glorified, took the keys of death, hell, and the grave, and then ascended. He had come as a Man from an extreme *glory zone*—the throne of God.

Just as sounds can travel through walls, you can travel through walls, too, because you are made of sound and glory. When you are in an extreme state of glory, the sound waves of your body can penetrate walls as they expand. Once the glory hits a certain level, it affects the sound waves inside your body and the entire molecular structure of your being.

How did Jesus and Peter walk on water? Jesus, who came in the form of a human like you and me, knew how to get into the glory realm, just as you and I can. The gravity and molecular structure of His body changed, and He became light enough in the glory to walk across the surface of the water.

Do you walk by the spirit, not the flesh? The flesh is your natural, carnal, worldly, and three-dimensional, limited way of thinking. Faith with action will get you into the glory realm of creative miracles faster than anything else—even if you don't understand it.

GRAVITY-DEFYING MIRACLES

Then it happened, as they continued on and talked, that suddenly a chariot of fire appeared with horses of fire, and separated the two of them; and Elijah went up by a whirlwind into heaven (2 Kings 2:11).

The Scriptures say that Jesus ascended in front of (at least) 500 of His disciples (see Acts 1:9), and that Elijah was taken up in a chariot of fire (see 2 Kings 2:11). Today there have been reports from various countries, including Argentina, about people levitating while preaching. If people involved in magic and sorcery, which draw from demonic power, can levitate and draw a crowd in broad daylight, as has been known to happen in New York City, how much more can the true children of God, blood-bought believers, move in even greater demonstrations of His power?

I truly believe that these examples from the Bible and recent history are foreshadows and glimpses of what the last-day church will look like and do for His glory and to display His power. Many seekers are now being seduced by demonic power camouflaged as pure and innocent as they search for the supernatural.

Will you rise to the occasion as Moses did with his rod, to challenge the current power and demonstrate an even greater power? Or will you, like many other followers of Jesus, shy away from the challenge and play it safe behind church walls every Sunday?

SOUNDS OF TRIUMPH

It shall come to pass, when they make a long blast with the ram's horn, and when you hear the sound of the trumpet, that all the people shall shout with a great shout; then the wall of the city will fall down flat. And the people shall go up every man straight before him (Joshua 6:5).

The walls of Jericho crumbled because people shouted—an amazing defiance of the law of gravity. What made the walls fall? The Israelites were told not to speak for one week. In this way they were conserving the power of the sound in their voices so on the day they released it their shouts would have greater power. It was as if a laser was concentrated on Jericho's walls—and down they came.

Words and sound contain certain levels of energy. If you say, "In the name of Jesus" with a tired voice and after having talked all day about nonsense, the power of your words is weakened. On the other hand, if you spend the day meditating on God and then speak, there is power in your words.

Can you imagine sounds loaded with the glory and power of God? There is a sound of God's glory that is released when you shout to the Lord corporately. Do you believe that sound is also energy and matter and that it has energy and weight to it? Do you believe that sound is a non-visible element but a very real object that, when in a concentrated form and filled with His glory, is a force to be reckoned with? What will you do with that knowledge?

END-TIME SUPERHEROES

Then Samson said: "With the jawbone of a donkey, heaps upon heaps, with the jawbone of a donkey I have slain a thousand men!" And so it was, when he had finished speaking, that he threw the jawbone from his hand... (Judges 15:16-17).

grew up watching Superman and other superheroes on television. Maybe these characters were inspired by biblical heroes. After all, Samson lifted the gates of an entire city. He killed a thousand men with the jawbone of a donkey, and did many other amazing feats. Elijah outran a chariot, and Philip was transported faster than a blink to another town to preach. Jesus demonstrated the first invisible cloaking device when He disappeared from the midst of a crowd ready to stone Him! They had rocks in their hands and were looking right at Jesus—the next moment, He was gone. (See Judges 16:3; First Kings 18:44-46; Acts 8:39-40; John 8:59; 10:39.)

Superhuman strength and power come from a supernatural God. The kind of miraculous things that happened from Genesis through Revelation can and will happen again. I believe that God is now releasing supernatural visions and accurate, detailed words of knowledge about things happening behind closed doors.

Is God equipping you as a superhero for Jesus who will heal and even resurrect the dead? Will you be one to take down demonic evil ones threatening cities and countries? The world is desperate for some "Glory Superheroes for Jesus."

While we wait for His return, are you willing to demonstrate the power of His love and redemption?

DAY 9
DREAMS, VISIONS, AND TRANCES

And it shall come to pass afterward that I will pour out My Spirit on all flesh; your sons and your daughters shall prophesy, your old men shall dream dreams, your young men shall see visions (Joel 2:28).

In these last days, I believe God is choosing to use dreams and visions as major means of speaking to His people, and giving direction and answers to prayer.

Dreams and visions differ. Dreams are usually more prophetic and symbolic, not usually literal. Visions are actual pictures of what will happen. Though dreams take more experience and maturity to interpret than visions, they often offer much more detail once interpreted. That is why it says in Joel that *"old men shall dream dreams,* [and] your *young men shall see visions."* It may take more maturity to understand dreams than visions—a picture can say a thousand words.

Often, upon awakening, I hear the voice of God or receive a vision. When you are resting, your mind is relaxed and able to receive from Heaven. When your mind is full of the cares of life, when God tries to speak to you, you unknowingly block it out because the "mailbox is full." When you are praying but fully awake, often it is still hard to see a vision or hear the voice of God because your mind is prayerfully active with many thoughts and concerns.

Before going to sleep, do you ask God to give you a dream? He will often grant your request, as you trust your faith for dreams and ask in faith. Also ask Him for visions while you are praying or soaking in His presence.

PRACTICING VISIONS

*After these things the word of the Lord came to Abram
in a vision, saying, "Do not be afraid, Abram. I am your
shield, your exceedingly great reward"* (Genesis 15:1).

You can practice receiving visions. Basically, we can all receive visions. They are simply pictures in your mind that God brings to you. Visions are not always accompanied with goose bumps, an angel, or an audible voice. More often than not, they are mental pictures God gives you, and you simply go with what you are seeing. *Seeing* is the essence of a vision.

Start to practice receiving visions, and write down the mental pictures you receive when you are praying, soaking, driving, or whenever you experience one. Then compare notes and see which ones are accurate so you can begin to hone the gift for His glory.

Trances are similar to visions or dreams but occur while you are in a sleeplike state. Often people call them daydreams. Some have been known to slip into a trance while driving and then wonder how they were able to drive and be lost in the trance at the same time.

Have you experienced a vision or a trance? Were you comforted, afraid, or did you experience a combination of the two? Will you welcome future experiences that God has for you?

DAY 11
GEOGRAPHICAL PORTALS TO HEAVEN

But I say to you, do not swear at all: neither by heaven, for it is God's throne; nor by the earth, for it is His footstool; nor by Jerusalem, for it is the city of the great King (Matthew 5:34-35).

There are some places on earth that already have an open portal to Heaven that makes it easier to receive revelation. For instance, when you are in a church or city that is experiencing revival, there is an open portal that allows a greater awareness of the supernatural—possibly a Jacob's ladder-type of portal with angels ascending and descending. The biggest portal is in Jerusalem. I believe it is the easiest place to hear from God, and to receive dreams and visions; angelic appearances are also common occurrences there.

Of all the cities in the world, the Lord has designated Jerusalem as His city—the city of the great King. That's not to mention the fact that Jesus died, was buried, and rose from the dead there and will return there. The first major revivals in the Book of Acts also took place in Jerusalem.

Satan tries to entrench himself in areas called to be great portals so as to keep them closed up and inaccessible. Sedona, Arizona, and Mecca in Saudi Arabia are said to be portals, but for darkness rather than Light. Are you sensitive to places where you feel the presence of God more than in others? Do you take advantage of this closeness to Him? How?

GREATER GLORY

*Then she [Elizabeth] spoke out with a loud voice and said,
"Blessed are you [Mary] among women, and blessed is
the fruit of your womb! But why is this granted to me, that
the mother of my Lord should come to me? For indeed,
as soon as the voice of your greeting sounded in my ears,
the babe leaped in my womb for joy"* (Luke 1:42-44).

The greater the glory, the quicker things will happen. Jesus prophesied that the centurion's servant would be healed and that very hour he was healed (see Matt. 8:5-13). Mary had received a prophecy from the angel of the Lord that she would be pregnant with Jesus (see Luke 1:26-38) and immediately she was pregnant.

These were glory-filled events—fresh from the throne of God. After a glory-filled prophecy is given, the only thing to do is believe it. That is very important. The greater the glory, the greater the miracles—but also the greater the judgment. There will be swift miracles, but also swift correction or judgment. Both will accelerate, depending on our response to God.

For example, Ananias and Sapphira were not honest. Because of their deception, Peter prophetically declared that they would die. Why is this sin so harshly and swiftly judged when surely there were greater sins in the New Testament church? Do you believe that God is not fooling around in these last days and that He won't allow people to counterfeit what He really wants to do?

DAY 13
STEPPING INTO
NEW REALMS

*"I am the vine, you are the branches. He who abides
in Me, and I in him, bears much fruit; for without
Me you can do nothing"* (John 15:5).

There is no limit in the glory. Prophecy sends angels on your behalf to arrange all kinds of things. One experience I had was flying into Washington, D.C. During the flight, the Lord told me that within the next few days I would be inside the White House praying for the nation at a very critical time. I could sense the unquestionable heavy weight of God's glory at the time. Since I was in the *glory zone*, I immediately declared what was told to me—that the doors are open to the White House.

In the natural, I did not know anyone with such connections; but within 24 hours of giving my social security number, and with the escort of a White House staff worker, I was cleared to go inside the White House and was given a private tour. I prayed in each of the important rooms where many decisions are made on a daily basis—decisions affecting our nation and the world.

"So I prophesied as I was commanded; and as I prophesied, there was a noise, and suddenly a rattling; and the bones came together, bone to bone" (Ezek. 37:7). The moment Ezekiel began to prophesy, the noise of rattling "suddenly" began and the miracle started.

How closely are you listening for the Lord's voice? How open are you to declare what He tells you as truth?

VIOLENT SOWING

May the Lord God of your fathers make you a thousand
times more numerous than you are, and bless you
as He has promised you! (Deuteronomy 1:11)

B efore we can walk in mighty reaping, there must be violent sowing. When the widow gave Elijah her last meal, it was a violent attack against the poverty, fear, and reality of her present circumstances. (See First Kings 17:8-15.) Such leaps of faith cause great reaping to take place.

When you sow sacrificially into a ministry that is moving in the glory and blessing of the Lord, God causes the same measure you have given plus the measure of glory that rests on that ministry to be multiplied supernaturally.

Should we give only to receive? No, we give because it is the highest act of worship. But at the same time, you give knowing that you will also receive. It's not the only reason to give, but it is one of the benefits. When you praise and worship God with songs, you do it out of love; yet you also believe for God's presence to come upon you in return. Is it selfish if your motives for receiving are good and for His glory? What farmer would go out sowing and then feel ashamed to reap what he has sown? This is how God created the order of things. How generously are you willing to give?

DAY 15

VIOLENT REAPING

*The kingdom of heaven suffers violence, and the
violent take it by force* (Matthew 11:12b).

Our level of obedience in sacrificial giving is totally connected to the level of the supernatural and the miraculous that God will entrust to us. The Bible clearly points out in Luke 16:12 and Luke 19:17 that if God cannot trust us to give our material riches when He asks for it, He certainly will not trust us with great spiritual riches. This is one reason many are not seeing the extraordinary miracles, salvations, and provisions as experienced in the Book of Acts.

Are you willing to free up yourself in this area of finances in order to see God's power resurrected in your day? How many times have you given an offering, and then weeks or months went by and you totally forgot about what you gave? You did not reap, and you wondered why the harvest was taking so long. You thought that God would just give you whatever was due you as He wills. How will you know if what you received was from your giving if you don't even remember what you gave?

The truth is, God is telling you to purposely start reaping the things He has promised you instead of receiving only what God spoon-feeds you. Are you prepared for violent reaping that starts with sowing violently and abundantly, and then looking for the harvest and purposely reaping it abundantly?

FAITH VERSUS HOPE

But do you want to know, O foolish man, that faith
without works is dead? (James 2:20)

How many times have you asked God to bless a certain project, hoping that the money would come in? You probably hoped God would do it, but you did not have full assurance that He would. There is a big difference between faith and hope. Faith is now; hope is future tense. If you hope for it, it's still out there in the future. When you know that you know it's done, it's a now thing. The reason for this is in the giving.

Have you given in such a way that when it came time for you to reap you had sown enough to reap what you were trying to receive? This is why it is important to keep track or at least have an idea of what you have sown in the glory. Usually when the giving requires a sacrifice, you remember it well. When it comes time for you to purchase that property or go on a mission trip, you know you have sown enough to reap it if God multiplies your giving.

How do you know when you are ready to reap? You know when supernatural faith enters in, and you know that you know God has done it—not by hoping and pleading, but simply by receiving what has already been done. When you take the *leap of faith*, God comes through. How many leaps of faith have you taken lately? Are you sitting back hoping rather than standing up leaping?

DAY 17
REAPING WHAT YOU
DID NOT SOW

*I have given you a land for which you did not labor, and cities which
you did not build, and you dwell in them; you eat of the vineyards
and olive groves which you did not plant* (Joshua 24:13).

After you have been faithful to sow sacrificially and then purposely reap what you sowed, you can enter the next dimension: *reaping where you did not sow*. This is the realm of living in the over and above, where you go beyond your cup being filled to where your cup is running over. Few enter this realm because they don't master the sacrificial sowing or the violent reaping dimension on a consistent basis.

This is where things get exciting.

The key is to declare it with your mouth, "I reap where I have never sowed." After you declare it out loud, angels are released to hearken to the Word of God. When you declare the Word, angels can't distinguish between your voice or God's because it is *His Word*. They react as if He Himself is declaring it. That is the authority that comes when you declare a revelation from Heaven.

Is your purpose and motive for entering this realm to be a blessing to others? Are you willing to purge yourself of any and all selfish desires to hoard or to follow certain principles of blessing out of a spirit of greed? The end result must be, "Lord, bless me so I can be a blessing to others and fulfill the call You have on my life."

REAPING THE WORLD'S WEALTH

A good man leaves an inheritance to his children's children, but the wealth of the sinner is stored up for the righteous (Proverbs 13:22).

The final and highest level of reaping in the material sense is reaping the wealth of the world or the sinner. In it is the greatest wealth for the Kingdom of God.

How do you reap from the world? The only way it works is if you sow into the earth that God created and the system that God put into place—I mean invest. God created the earth to produce, and the world is profiting off of the system that God put into place. Believers who do not invest in the present world can't reap from it.

I believe that God wants the world's money to work for you, instead of you working for the world's money. Ask a trusted and credible financial or banking consultant for advice. You may receive a prophetic direction to invest, for example, in a certain stock or real estate. Months later, the stock may skyrocket and God may tell you to sell the shares you bought or your real estate—God blesses your obedience.

Unfortunately, many of God's people are in financial bondage and debt. Are you consistently asking God for a prophetic word and direction about how to get out of your famine and into His blessing? Do you trust in and know that He is the same God today as the God who provided for Elijah more than 2,000 years ago? He continually cares about every area of your life, including your finances.

RECIPE FOR REAPING

The Lord will open to you His good treasure, the heavens, to give the rain to your land in its season, and to bless all the work of your hand. You shall lend to many nations, but you shall not borrow (Deuteronomy 28:12).

I strongly suggest that you use this recipe for financial success and stability:

1. Give your tithes to God so He will protect you from the devourer.

2. Sow and reap abundantly into the glory.

3. Put at least 10 percent aside into a savings account or somewhere safe until you are ready to invest it.

4. Try to save at least three months' worth of living expenses as a job-loss buffer.

5. Invest and multiply the "leftover" money.

6. Sow again some of the money you reaped into ministries that are good ground. That way you are reaping from your giving into the Kingdom and reaping the wealth of the world at the same time. By doing this, you will have more and more with which to bless God.

Some Christians wrongly surmise that it is a sin to be blessed materially. The root of this belief comes from anti-Semitism. As believers come back to loving and supporting Israel and the Jewish people, who preserved the oracles and Word of God for the world, a double portion of blessing will also return to us as we tap into the rich and fertile promises of God.

Does this recipe look like something you want to follow? How deeply in debt are you willing to go before trying this recipe? Can it realistically be applied to your current situation? Why or why not?

DAY 20
BEING A VOICE

I have been crucified with Christ; it is no longer I who live, but Christ lives in me; and the life which I now live in the flesh I live by faith in the Son of God, who loved me and gave Himself for me (Galatians 2:20).

Your identity has to be so changed that you don't look at your own stature, influence, or past identity. You must have a total transformation of identity, which comes from being transformed by the presence and glory of Jesus. Peter had a total change of identity because he had been with Jesus. He boldly confronted the religious leaders, telling them to repent and that it was they who crucified the Lord (see Acts 4:5-12). They were amazed at his boldness and authority, knowing he was unlearned and a simple fisherman from Galilee. His past identity did not stop Peter. In Matthew 4:19, Jesus gave him a new identity, "fisher of men!"

Lay down everything you think you are or are not in the eyes of others, and let God resurrect you into a new creation. As you start to see yourself in His eyes and act that way, others will recognize a new authority in you, and you will become a new person.

Paul's identity was changed when he encountered the glory on the road to Damascus. He was blinded for three days and was a changed man. One powerful experience in His glory will change you and blind you to what you were, and open your eyes to a new calling and identity. Do you too frequently remember the old you? Are you stuck in the past—a past that God has already forgotten?

DAY 21
WHAT KINGS LOOK FOR

He who gets wisdom loves his own soul; he who cherishes understanding prospers (Proverbs 19:8 NIV).

"Kings" can be government leaders as well as business executives, community and school officials, famous entertainers, religious leaders, or any person who has major influence over a nation, community, or people group.

Kings of the earth look for an Elijah who has a message or direction from God to answer their questions or solve their problems. You can be nice, polite, and politically correct, but if you don't have a Word from God and a solution, kings will soon realize that you are wasting their time. One word from God changes it all.

Get in the spirit, flow in the glory of God, and listen for a Word from God—gain wisdom from Him. That is your main weapon that you can't leave home without. Although you may be able to quote all the Scriptures, make sure God has spoken to you before approaching a king.

Many times, kings search out those who can counsel and direct them in the right path through the supernatural. Many leaders consult mediums, psychics, or sorcerers. Have you consulted these types of "counselors" rather than seeking God's Word? Do you know others who depend on these types of sources for direction? What advice do you have for them?

DAY 22
MOTIVES

So it was, when Elisha the man of God heard that the king of Israel had torn his clothes, that he sent to the king, saying, "Why have you torn your clothes? Please let him come to me, and he shall know that there is a prophet in Israel" (2 Kings 5:8).

Leaders look for someone who is trustworthy and without ulterior motives. When the Syrian army commander Naaman offered to give many material treasures to Elisha in gratitude for being healed of leprosy, the prophet refused them because God had told him not to take them. Maybe Naaman attempted to pay for the healing he received from Elisha's God because he had paid sorcerers in the past for their services. He may have believed that this relieved him of any debt that he owed God and the man of God.

But Naaman's only debt to the Lord God of Israel was worship. Elisha's servant, though, went back, lied to Naaman, pretended that Elisha had changed his mind and wanted the material rewards, and took them for himself, thus compromising his character and showing that he was a double-minded man. (See Second Kings 5:20-27.)

So first, you need a word from God; and second, you need to be trustworthy. Being trustworthy is especially important when it concerns private or sensitive issues. Can you discern between a gift given to you as unto God in thanksgiving, and a gift given to you by someone with a control element, with the motivation of securing future words when needed, or given as payment for your help?

STEPPING INTO GOVERNMENT GLORY

And so we have the prophetic word confirmed, which you do well to heed as a light that shines in a dark place, until the day dawns and the morning star rises in your hearts (2 Peter 1:19).

I have learned the importance of upgrading prophetic gifts. Many are satisfied with the beginner's stage of the prophetic, for example, simply describing a prophetic vision: "I see a vision, the sky is blue, you are in a boat, and the wind is blowing." And then when someone asks what it could mean, you respond by stating you don't know, but that is what you saw.

When God puts someone of high authority in your path, and the destiny and direction of a nation, community, or organization could be at stake, it's time to believe God for more detailed words that a leader will quickly identify as being from God. I believe that within the church God provides a safe environment to grow in the gifts, but when it's time to use them in the world, that is the time to demonstrate the power of God and the upgraded prophetic gifting.

How comfortable are you to share with another a word that God has given to you?

DAY 24
GATEWAYS

*So the field of Ephron [was] deeded to Abraham as a
possession in the presence of the sons of Heth, before all
who went in at the gate of his city* (Genesis 23:17-18).

If God tells you to speak to government or other leaders, then declare this prophetically to yourself; as you do, God will send angels, people, and circumstances to make the arrangements.

As I was flying to preach in Wanganui, New Zealand, the Lord told me to prophesy that the gates of the city were opened. So I declared that the gates of the city were open to the Lord for the glory of God to come in.

There is a connection between ports of entry into a nation or city and the leaders or elders meeting you at the ports of entry. That day, both the pastor (the spiritual gate) and the mayor (the political gate) met me at the airport (the physical gate).

If you are faithful to pray and even fast for the world, governments, and citywide leaders whom God puts on your heart, the Lord may very well open the door for you to speak into those situations. Do you believe that God may use your prayers to open the way for you to give the Word of the Lord to leaders in desperate need? How likely do you think that situation may arise?

LET THERE BE LIGHT

Then Jesus spoke to them again, saying, "I am the light of the world. He who follows Me shall not walk in darkness, but have the light of life" (John 8:12).

Light expels darkness by its very nature. When the lights are on, there is no darkness. If you try to cast away darkness but you yourself are not full of light, chances are it will take you a long time to do it.

More and more, we need to learn to operate in the glory realm His way and to let His hand touch the people. Often we get in the way, wanting to do all the work when He can do it so much better and faster—with longer-lasting results. Ask God to use you in deliverance glory, to see not just people but also entire cities and nations freed from darkness into His glory.

When the glory comes, do you act, obey, and let God do what He intends to do in that glory? Do you keep praising until the spirit of worship comes? Do you feel more like loving on God, singing intimate slow songs of love to Him? Don't stop short of the greater glory of God and settle for something lightweight.

DAY 26
FASTING

*"Bring all the tithes into the storehouse, that there may
be food in My house, and try Me now in this," says the
Lord of hosts, "if I will not open for you the windows of
heaven and pour out for you such blessing that there will
not be room enough to receive it"* (Malachi 3:10).

Fasting propels your spirit into the glory much like the rocket
boosters and the enormous power that propels a space shuttle into
orbit. Once in that realm, you tend to hear God better, the power and
presence of God increases upon you, and your faith deepens if you are
spending that time in prayer, praise, and the Word. Your spirit is totally
focused on the spirit realm and distractions tend to lose their grip.

That is why Jesus, the apostles, Moses, Elijah, and most of the
patriarchs led a life of fasting and prayer with such phenomenal
results that they shook nations and saw impossibilities become realities. Another key to ushering in the glory is *sacrificial giving*.

Are fasting, prayer, and sacrificial giving a regular part of your
lifestyle? What glory and miracles may you be missing if you are not
willing to spend time fasting, praying, and giving? How many windows
of Heaven can be opened to you if you propel your spirit into glory?

WHEN THE SPIRIT MOVES

In the beginning God created the heavens and the earth.
The earth was without form and void; and darkness
was on the face of the deep. And the Spirit of God was
hovering over the face of the waters (Genesis 1:1-2).

Our sensitivity to God's moving needs to be developed. As soon as the Spirit began to move over the waters in the Book of Genesis, then God spoke in verse 3: *"'Let there be light'; and there was light."* We have to wait until the Spirit moves before we declare the prophetic, pray for miracles, or take great steps of faith. After the Spirit has moved, then you step out in faith and do or say that which God is doing or saying while He is moving. After the presence of God's glory has moved, you can be sure that God has already gone before you to perform what you will say or do. Now you can pick the fruit.

During a service at a large African church in London, I told the people that the Spirit was moving and that anyone who was sick or needed a miracle should get up and run. Hundreds of people got up and started running—tumors dissolved, gold teeth fillings appeared, and many other miracles occurred.

When the Spirit moves, do you move with it? If the Spirit moves on you to do something or call someone, pray for someone, or give to someone, will you do it? Do so if you want miraculous results.

HOW TO INVITE THE SPIRIT TO MOVE

And when they had prayed, the place where they were assembled together was shaken; and they were all filled with the Holy Spirit, and they spoke the word of God with boldness (Acts 4:31).

Is there anything you can do to facilitate the moving of the Spirit? Is there anything you can do while you are waiting for Him to move to speed things up? Yes! Keep doing whatever you did to get Him to come in the first place, and soon you will sense when He is moving.

While you are waiting, praise, fast, pray, give, etc. until He moves. This is a discipline that will train your spiritual senses so you can discern the slightest moving of His Spirit.

Paul and Silas were in prison and needed the Spirit to move on their behalf. They continued praising Him until the glory and Spirit of God came. When the Spirit moved, they knew it! (See Acts 16:16-26.) In Acts 4:29-31, Peter and John and other believers kept praying, praising, fasting, and seeking God as they had done at Pentecost in Acts 2, and *"the place where they were assembled together was shaken; and they were all filled with the Holy Spirit"* (Acts 4:31). How consistent are your prayers, praise, and fasting?

NOT DEAD, ONLY SLEEPING

*Our friend Lazarus sleeps, but I go that I
may wake him up* (John 11:11b).

How could Jesus tell the Jews that Lazarus was not dead, when clearly, by all human measures, he was as dead as any other corpse? What was the revelation behind this, and how did He raise him from the dead? Earlier in the passage, Jesus even had said that Lazarus' sickness was not unto death but for the glory of God (see verse 4).

One day while I was preaching in one of our miracle campaigns, this revelation hit me right before I went up to the microphone—Jesus was able to speak to Lazarus even though he was physically dead. How was Jesus able to speak to him? Because Lazarus knew Jesus! After the life of Jesus touches a life and breathes on it, it can never die. Because you have a living, personal relationship with the Messiah, you will never die.

Anything that God has breathed upon that seems dead is actually not dead but only sleeping or in a spiritual coma! Has God spoken or prophesied some things over your life that once had life and now seem dead? Did God use you powerfully in a certain way and now it seems to be lost or gone? Those gifts and prophecies are not dead.

Why do you think Paul reminded Timothy to *"stir up"* the gift that was in him? (See Second Timothy 1:5-7.)

DAY 30
THE SAME YESTERDAY, TODAY, AND TOMORROW

Jesus said to her, "I am the resurrection and the life. He who believes in Me, though he may die, he shall live" (John 11:25).

Across the United States, Europe, and many other Western nations, the abundant glory and power of God is once again resurrecting and waking up what was and continues to be.

Several years ago I ministered in Spokane, Washington, where John G. Lake had ministered healing to the whole city. People came to his healing rooms and everyone who entered left healed.

The glory that touched the city and seemed to have faded away is actually sleeping, waiting for someone else to wake it up. A short time later I learned that someone had bought the property and renamed it the "healing rooms" and the healing ministry of John G. Lake is continuing today right where it started! After God has breathed on an area, a city, a ministry, or anything, it only sleeps; it never dies. Wake it up!

Are you eager to stir up the gifts in you and stir up the mantles over your region? Are you looking forward to God unleashing the *Elijah glory* with resurrection power to raise bodies, ministries, families, and nations from the dead?

RESURRECTION GLORY AND ISRAEL

Therefore prophesy and say to them, "Thus says the Lord God: 'Behold, O My people, I will open your graves and cause you to come up from your graves, and bring you back into the land of Israel. Then you shall know that I am the Lord, when I have opened your graves, O My people, and brought you up from your graves. I will put My Spirit in you and you shall live, and I will place you in your own land. Then you shall know that I, the Lord, have spoken it and performed it,' says the Lord" (Ezekiel 37:12-14).

Wow, what an exciting time we live in! This passage says that God is opening the graves of the Jewish people and bringing them back to their land, Israel. Many Jews are moving to Israel, but there are many more who want and need to go home to Israel.

I believe that in this next and maybe final move of God, any ministry or believer who does not have some type of emphasis on blessing and praying for Israel, sharing the Messiah, or loving Israel and the Jewish people in these last days, will begin to notice a dwindling of influence and a loss of their anointing, favor, and finances. For those who don't connect, death and stagnation will occur.

Do you pray for the peace of Jerusalem? Do you believe what Psalm 122:6b-7 says about Jerusalem? *"May they prosper who love you. Peace be within your walls, prosperity within your palaces."*

THE MASTER KEY TO THE DOUBLE PORTION

For the gifts and the calling of God are irrevocable (Romans 11:29).

I have noticed something important about those who walk with the greatest mantles—they also honor Israel and the Jewish people, who are the spiritual parents of all believers. As we honor our spiritual parents, Israel and the Jewish people, God promises a special blessing. In fact, in these last days those who do not honor Israel will not receive the double portion.

The restoration of the spirit of Elijah is connected to the hearts of the fathers (Israel) turning to their children, and the children (the Church) to their fathers. (See Malachi 4:5-6.) How can we receive a double portion of what the early church had if we don't identify, honor, and associate ourselves with the Jews? The restoration of the spirit of Elijah requires us to stand firm with Israel in her time of crises—even when it is not popular to do so.

If we cut ourselves off from identifying with the Jewish people, we lose that generational blessing, and are cut off from the root of where the blessings began. The blessings came out of Abraham and the Jewish people. Have you re-plugged yourself into that root of blessings that started with Abraham and continued all the way to Jesus, the early church, and the Church today? Are you willing to take a strong stand with your forefather Israel and see the inheritance and double portion come upon you? Pray for Israel and the Jewish people—for their salvation, protection, and return to their land.

JUDEO-CHRISTIAN HERITAGE

*Do not boast against the branches. But if you do
boast, remember that you do not support the root,
but the root supports you* (Romans 11:18).

The only reason God blessed and favored Esther was so she could use this favor to bless Israel (see Esther 4:14). If she failed, she would have missed the reason for her existence—blessed to be a blessing to Israel. We, too, must reveal our true identity as children of God and offspring of Israel.

The nations that have experienced great revival in Christendom are among the most blessed and respected nations in the world. Will America and her allies stand by Israel and the Jews, knowing that their blessings originated when they helped Israel become a nation again and a refuge for many Jews? Or will we close our eyes and try to be politically correct so as to possibly avoid future enemy attacks? If we don't take a strong stand with that which initiated our blessing, we will eventually lose what we are trying to save. We must stand with the root of our blessings and spiritual inheritance instead of cutting off our root system in hopes of self-preservation.

Will you be silent in these days when it is unpopular to stand with Israel and the Jewish people; or will you reveal that you are one with Israel, honor your spiritual fathers of the faith and Jesus Himself, who came as a Jew?

NEW GLORIES

See, I have this day set you over the nations and over the kingdoms, to root out and to pull down, to destroy and to throw down, to build and to plant (Jeremiah 1:10).

There are new waves and manifestations of God's glory that have yet to be manifested on the earth. The new glories will only be manifested as nations untouched by God's glory are awakened. The Middle East and Arab nations have not yet seen the awesome glory that will be revealed once God wakes up those sleeping giants. China saw a tremendous glory and reproduced millions of new converts in a short amount of time once the glory invaded that nation. Israel and the world will experience the greatest end-time glory invasion when the King of Glory, the Messiah, comes and takes His place in Jerusalem.

God often sends His people from one nation to another to help those nations dig deep and discover His treasures hidden deep in the soil. I believe that churches and believers who cannot go to other nations, but instead pray and help send others with their finances, will also walk in the glory invasion and partake of a greater glory of God in their lives. When pressing into His glory, are you asking Him to release a *glory invasion of God* in your life and accelerating what He wants to do through you?

YOUR MIND AND THOUGHTS

...Know the God of your father, and serve Him with a loyal heart and with a willing mind; for the Lord searches all hearts and understands all the intent of the thoughts. If you seek Him, He will be found by you; but if you forsake Him, He will cast you off forever (1 Chronicles 28:9).

Just as you are what you eat, you also are what you think. The way you see yourself is who you become. Every action is based first on a thought. Once your thoughts start to change—about yourself and life—your life starts to change. Actions are the results of thoughts. To see change, you need to allow your thoughts to be conditioned. Take control of your thoughts and do not allow just any thoughts to dominate your life. Just as raw food has an energy force, thoughts are so powerful that they release energy—good or bad—depending on the thought.

When you have a strange dream of someone trying to hurt you, your heart beats faster and you wake up feeling exhausted, as if it really happened. Your mind treated it as fact. As you see images in your mind or on a movie screen, your body reacts to them positively or negatively.

Are you living in a constant state of fear and anxiety, which depletes your immune system? Will you commit to thinking about things that are helpful, exciting, positive, and energizing?

DAY 36
VISUALIZATION

For as he thinks in his heart, so is he... (Proverbs 23:7).

When you see yourself as achieving great health and joy, thinking the best of people, and having other positive thoughts, these thoughts release a rejuvenation of your cells, and your health improves. If you start to see yourself in great internal and external shape, your mind will send a signal to your body that helps you achieve this or any other goal.

If you think there is no way, then that is what you will get. Most sickness can be a result of wrong thinking that leads to wrong actions about food choices or emotional patterns, which in turn lead to sickness. You need to take full control of what you allow to enter your mind. If it is a negative thought, quickly replace it with a positive thought of someone who told you that he or she loved you, or when your baby was born, or anything positive that happened in your life.

You have to take negative thoughts captive and then send them on their way.

Everything you see around you was first created in someone's mind and then came into manifested reality. You are what you think about and how you see yourself. How do you see yourself? Do you have a positive attitude about yourself? What are you visualizing about yourself right now?

OVERCOMING PAST THOUGHTS

...If your brother sins against you, rebuke him; and if he repents, forgive him. And if he sins against you seven times in a day, and seven times in a day returns to you, saying, "I repent," you shall forgive him (Luke 17:3-4).

How do you get rid of negative thoughts that have been there since your youth? Many people have been negatively conditioned as kids by parents, teachers, and other authority figures—even other classmates.

To change wrong thinking, take charge of your life and do not let someone else dictate who you are. The most powerful force in the world is forgiveness; forgive people who hurt you so you can go forward to create a new future. Continuing to hold on to what someone said or did, as bad as it was at the time, limits you and becomes self-destructive.

Once you forgive, it will feel like a million pounds of weight lifted off of you—freeing you from a prison of defeat into a new life of limitless possibilities. Try it right now and simply say, "I forgive so-and-so from what he or she did or said to me." Say it several times to imprint it into your psyche and spirit.

Now you are on your way to supernatural health,. as this is the most powerful thing you could ever do! Can you imagine a lifestyle where people notice a new joy and are attracted to you because of a sense of love and forgiveness that will exude from you?

DAY 38
FOCUS

Whatever things are true, whatever things are noble, whatever things are just, whatever things are pure, whatever things are lovely, whatever things are of good report, if there is any virtue and if there is anything praiseworthy—meditate on these things (Philippians 4:8).

Focus on things that are noble and positive.

You always move toward what you focus on. Focus on how you will feel when you achieve this or that dream or goal. Once you start to imagine how you will feel, you actually will tap into the joy and satisfaction of a future event before it happens. Your mind and body can't always tell if what you are thinking is in the present or future, but start to cause your body, spirit, and everything else to react now—according to the positive goal you are thinking about, whether it be present, future, or past.

As you strongly focus more on what you are aiming for, your brain will start to work overtime to find the solution in your subconscious while you sleep. Clear your mind of fear and worry so that you can make room for the solutions that will come to you once you create the proper environment to receive them. Your mind is like a memory card that only has so much memory on it. Is your mind full of stress and negative things? How quickly can you delete it all and receive a fresh download from above?

DESIRE

*When He had called the people to Himself, with His disciples also,
He said to them, "Whoever desires to come after Me, let him deny
himself, and take up his cross, and follow Me"* (Mark 8:34).

What you think about often leads to stronger desires. When you couple consistent thinking and desire, they start to manifest into reality. The stronger your desire, the faster you will act on it. Again, it all starts with thoughts. If you *casually* desire to be in good health but are not motivated enough to act on it, then your desire needs to be increased to spur you to action. If you *strongly* desire chocolate chip cookies because of a television commercial, you may run to the store and buy some.

As mentioned previously, thoughts and visuals have an effect on your body, mind, and spirit. See your future and destiny favorably and think positively about your life. Believe in the truth that God has a perfect plan for you—believe it. Are you willing to think this way on a consistent basis attracting the necessities, connections, and resources to fulfill your God-given destiny?

DAY 40
CREATING YOUR FUTURE

Then Jesus said to them, "When you lift up the Son of Man, then you will know that I am He, and that I do nothing of Myself; but as My Father taught Me, I speak these things" (John 8:28).

What you speak has an amazing effect on everything you do and on your body. Speech is so powerful that the Book of Genesis records that everything was created by it. In the beginning, the Creator spoke, *"Let there be light' and there was light"* (Gen. 1:3). Speech and sounds that you speak or make, though invisible to the naked eye, are real objects. If an opera singer can sing at a high pitch and break glass, then a sound wave is a tiny, invisible object—like a pebble—but much smaller. At high speeds or frequencies, it can pierce through another object.

Everything created on this earth is made up of core subatomic particles that can be altered by human observation—amazing! Just thinking about certain things immediately causes either a positive or negative effect on your body, whether angry thoughts releasing poisons, or happy, loving thoughts releasing healing. Whatever you think about and speak starts to be created. You become what you think and speak about.

How conscious are you about the words you speak? Are your words piercing someone's heart? Are your words lifting someone's confidence?

DAVID HERZOG MINISTRIES

D avid Herzog is the founder of David Herzog Ministries. He and his wife, Stephanie, are hosts of "The Glory Zone," a weekly television program, which is aired in the United States on GOD TV. David and Stephanie have ministered in crusades, conferences, revivals, and outreaches throughout the United States, Canada, England, Scotland, Ireland, France, Germany, Switzerland, Belgium, Italy, Spain, Denmark, Holland, Norway, Malta, Africa, Australia, New Zealand, New Caledonia, Mexico, French Guiana, Madagascar, Papua New Guinea, the Caribbean, the Arctic, Native American reservations, Kuwait, and Israel. They have also lived 12 years overseas ministering to the nations of the world. The Herzogs have led 12 tours/outreaches to Israel.

David is a prophetic evangelist and motivational speaker who moves in miracles and trains believers worldwide to operate in the glory and power of God and to succeed in every area of their lives. His desire is to create a center to train people to do great works while taking the Gospel around the world via television, crusades, revival meetings, and prophetic street evangelism. The Herzogs are based in Sedona, Arizona, where they live with their three daughters.

Supporting the greater cause of reaching the harvest of souls worldwide connects you to a glory and breakthrough greater than what you can accomplish on your own. Together, believers accomplish many times more. When you give into a ministry that is good ground and lives in the *glory zone* that reaches the harvest, God blesses and multiplies what you give exponentially.

Partners allow the David Herzog Ministries to go beyond and accomplish many times over what they could with their own gifts, strength, or finances. The ministry travels around the world to reach the lost through crusades, mission trips, revivals, and feeding the poor. The worldwide television program, "The Glory Zone," airs now on every continent. The ministry strongly supports Israel by outreaches and giving generously to ministries that feed the poor. Each year hundreds of people travel to Israel and pray for her revival.

Dear Reader,

We invite you to be part of our family and enter into the shared blessings of partnering with us to take the Gospel to all people. Presently, our television program is bringing in many souls and opening doors to hold evangelistic campaigns in many hard-to-enter countries. As you give and pray, we believe that you will receive a portion of the same favor, glory, and mantle that has been placed on this ministry. If you feel this ministry is good glory ground in which to sow, please consider becoming a partner by giving a monthly donation or a larger, one-time gift to spread the Gospel to the ends of the earth.

To become a partner, visit us online at: www.thegloryzone.org.

Or write to us at:

David Herzog Ministries
PO Box 2070
Sedona, AZ 86339
USA

Invite David Herzog to Your Area

David Herzog may be available to speak at your church, conference, or crusade. Please contact us with details of your invitation and the nature of the event. David and his team will pray over your invitation and respond to you as soon as possible.

Watch "The Glory Zone" on Television Each Week

For more information, go to www.thegloryzone.com.

Receive these publications that contain news about upcoming meetings and outreaches near you, information about new products, and updates on the latest videos from our television program and outreaches. For more information about our ministry, or to sign up for free, weekly e-mail news and information, visit www.thegloryzone.org.

BOOKS AND RESOURCES
BY DAVID HERZOG

Mysteries of the Glory Unveiled ($15.00 plus $3.00 S&H)

Fifty years after the last great miracle revival, believers of every Christian denomination are beginning to experience this restoration of what the author calls "the former and latter rains of Glory." As foretold by the prophets, this rain is resulting in the greatest harvest of souls the world has ever known.

What took centuries to understand and accomplish, God is doing in an instant in this present glory. God is now unveiling the mysteries of His glory to hungry believers who seek the knowledge of His glory.

Desperate for New Wine ($15.00 plus $3.00 S&H)

One New Year's Eve, the Lord challenged me to write this book as a blessing to God's people and as a tool to spread this move of the Holy Spirit from renewal to revival. While focusing our sights not only on renewal but also on where it is going on a global scale, I decided to obey Him. Much of the content and many of the principles in this book were given to me by the Lord as revelation, especially during times of fasting and prayer. The other parts are based on our experiences with the new wine of His Spirit as we are seeing renewal and revival occur in various nations where we minister. This book gives you an understanding of our crucial current times and will inspire you to seize this moment in history as your own for His glory.

DVDs (All DVDs $15 plus $3.00 S&H)

Each DVD is filled with teachings and testimonies of miracles.

* *Walking Under an Open Heaven*
* *Miracles in the Glory*
* *Israel and the Glory*
* *How to Do Miracles*
* And many more!

Order online at www.thegloryzone.org or write to:

DHM
PO Box 2070
Sedona, AZ 86339

In the right hands, This Book will Change Lives!

Most of the people who need this message will not be looking for this book. To change their lives, you need to put a copy of this book in their hands.

> But others (seeds) fell into good ground, and brought forth fruit, some a hundred-fold, some sixty-fold, some thirty-fold (Matthew 13:8).

Our ministry is constantly seeking methods to find the good ground, the people who need this anointed message to change their lives. Will you help us reach these people?

> Remember this—a farmer who plants only a few seeds will get a small crop. But the one who plants generously will get a generous crop (2 Corinthians 9:6).

EXTEND THIS MINISTRY BY SOWING
3 BOOKS, 5 BOOKS, 10 BOOKS, OR MORE TODAY,
AND BECOME A LIFE CHANGER!

Thank you,

Don Nori Sr., Founder
Destiny Image
Since 1982

DESTINY IMAGE PUBLISHERS, INC.

"Promoting Inspired Lives."

VISIT OUR NEW SITE HOME AT
WWW.DESTINYIMAGE.COM

FREE SUBSCRIPTION TO DI NEWSLETTER

Receive free unpublished articles by top DI authors, exclusive
discounts, and free downloads from our best and newest books.

Visit www.destinyimage.com to subscribe.

Write to: Destiny Image
              P.O. Box 310
              Shippensburg, PA 17257-0310

Call: 1-800-722-6774

Email: orders@destinyimage.com

For a complete list of our titles or to place an order
online, visit www.destinyimage.com.

FIND US ON FACEBOOK OR FOLLOW US ON TWITTER.

www.facebook.com/destinyimage   facebook
www.twitter.com/destinyimage   twitter